TITLES
AND FORMS OF ADDRESS

A GUIDE TO CORRECT USE

EIGHTEENTH EDITION

A & C BLACK
LONDON

© 1985 A. AND C. BLACK (PUBLISHERS) LTD
35 BEDFORD ROW LONDON WC1R 4JH

First Edition	1918	*Eleventh Edition*	1961
Second Edition	1929	*Twelfth Edition*	1964
Third Edition	1932	*Thirteenth Edition*	1966
Fourth Edition	1936	*Reprinted*	1969
Fifth Edition	1939	*Fourteenth Edition*	1971
Sixth Edition	1945	*Reprinted*	1972
Seventh Edition	1949	*Fifteenth Edition*	1976
Eighth Edition	1951	*Sixteenth Edition*	1978
Ninth Edition	1955	*Seventeenth Edition*	1980
Tenth Edition	1958	*Eighteenth Edition*	1985

British Library Cataloguing in Publication Data

Titles and forms of address: a guide to correct
use.—18th ed.
1. Forms of address   2. Titles of honor and
nobility.
395'.4   CR3515

ISBN 0-7136-2694-1

ISBN 0-7136-2694-1

TEXT SET IN 10/12 PT VIP BASKERVILLE, PRINTED AND BOUND
IN GREAT BRITAIN AT THE PITMAN PRESS, BATH

INTRODUCTION

The correct use of titles, and other distinguishing marks of honour or of office, has generally become established over a long period through the usage followed by the title-holders themselves and by those associated with them. Similarly, and very gradually, there occur modifications and changes in practice.

It seems desirable to point out that while great formality may from time to time be appropriate, and the forms to be used in such cases are therefore given, it will more often be proper to use simpler forms, as indicated throughout, in ordinary correspondence whether business or social.

It should be made clear that etiquette is a different subject and is not touched upon in this book.

The publishers are grateful to correspondents who have kindly suggested additions and improvements. At the same time they are bound to say that they are unable to provide an advisory or information service.

1985

CONTENTS

Contents

Contents

Contents

ABBREVIATIONS

This list consists solely of abbreviations which may be used after the name; it includes lettering ranging from orders and decorations which are used on all occasions to fellowships or memberships which would normally be used only in a professional context. Such lettering is frequently used on letterheads or cards, in lists and so on, and it is helpful to know what interests or qualifications it identifies; pages 178-82 give the rules by which the order of the various categories is determined. The list includes abbreviations used in the Commonwealth and the United States as well as in the United Kingdom. It is not, of course, comprehensive, but covers all such examples as have come to the attention of the editors.

A

AA	Augustinians of the Assumption
AASA	Associate, Australian Society of Accountants
AAUQ	Associate in Accountancy, University of Queensland
AB	Bachelor of Arts (US)
ABIA	Associate, Bankers' Institute of Australasia
ABINZ	Associate, Bankers' Institute of New Zealand
ABPsS	Associate, British Psychological Society
ABSM	Associate, Birmingham and Midland Institute School of Music
AC	Companion of the Order of Australia
ACA	Associate, Institute of Chartered Accountants
ACBSI	Associate, Chartered Building Societies Institute
ACCA	Associate, Association of Certified Accountants
ACCS	Associate, Corporation of Secretaries (*formerly* of Certified Secretaries)
ACGI	Associate, City and Guilds of London Institute
ACIArb	Associate, Chartered Institute of Arbitrators
ACII	Associate, Chartered Insurance Institute
ACIS	Associate, Institute of Chartered Secretaries and Administrators (*formerly* Chartered Institute of Secretaries)
ACIT	Associate, Chartered Institute of Transport
ACMA	Associate, Institute of Cost and Management Accountants
ACP	Associate, College of Preceptors
ACSM	Associate, Camborne School of Mines
ACT	Associate, College of Technology
AD	Dame of the Order of Australia
ADC	Aide-de-camp
ADCM	Archbishop of Canterbury's Diploma in Church Music
ADC(P)	Personal Aide-de-camp to HM The Queen
ADFManc	Art and Design Fellow, Manchester
ADK	Order of Ahli Darjah Kinabalu
AE	Air Efficiency Award
AEM	Air Efficiency Medal
AFAIAA	Associate Fellow, American Institute of Aeronautics and Astronautics
AFC	Air Force Cross
AFCAI	Associate Fellow, Canadian Aeronautical Institute
AFD	Doctor of Fine Arts (US)
AFIA	Associate, Federal Institute of Accountants (Australia)
AFICD	Associate Fellow, Institute of Civil Defence
AFIMA	Associate Fellow, Institute of Mathematics and its Applications
AFM	Air Force Medal

AFOM	Associate, Faculty of Occupational Medicine
AGI	Associate, Institute of Certificated Grocers
AGSM	Associate, Guildhall School of Music and Drama
AHA	Associate, Institute of Health Service Administrators
AH-WC	Associate, Heriot-Watt College, Edinburgh
AIA	Associate, Institute of Actuaries
AIAgrE	Associate, Institution of Agricultural Engineers
AIAL	Associate Member, International Institute of Arts and Letters
AIAS	Associate Surveyor Member, Incorporated Association of Architects and Surveyors
AIB	Associate, Institute of Bankers
AIBD	Associate, Institute of British Decorators
AIBP	Associate, Institute of British Photographers
AICE	Associate, Institution of Civil Engineers
AICS	Associate, Institute of Chartered Shipbrokers
AICTA	Associate, Imperial College of Tropical Agriculture
AIEE	Associate, Institution of Electrical Engineers
AIIA	Associate, Insurance Institute of America
AIInfSc	Associate, Institute of Information Scientists
AIL	Associate, Institute of Linguists
AILocoE	Associate, Institution of Locomotive Engineers
AIMarE	Associate, Institute of Marine Engineers
AInstM	Associate Member, Institute of Marketing
AInstPI	Associate, Institute of Patentees and Inventors
AIProdE	Associate, Institution of Production Engineers
AIQS	Associate Member, Institute of Quantity Surveyors
AIRTE	Associate, Institute of Road Transport Engineers
AISA	Associate, Incorporated Secretaries' Association
AIStructE	Associate, Institution of Structural Engineers
AK	Knight of the Order of Australia
AKC	Associate, King's College London
ALA	Associate, Library Association
ALAA	Associate, Library Association of Australia
ALAM	Associate, London Academy of Music and Dramatic Art
ALCD	Associate, London College of Divinity
ALCM	Associate, London College of Music
ALI	Associate, Landscape Institute
ALS	Associate, Linnean Society
AM	Albert Medal; Member of the Order of Australia; Master of Arts (US)
AMA	Associate of the Museums Association
AMCT	Associate, Manchester College of Technology
AMet	Associate of Metallurgy
AMIAE	Associate Member, Institution of Automobile Engineers
AMIAgrE	Associate Member, Institution of Agricultural Engineers

AMIBF	Associate Member, Institute of British Foundrymen
AMIChemE	Associate Member, Institution of Chemical Engineers
AMIE(Aust)	Associate Member, Institution of Engineers, Australia
AMIED	Associate Member, Institution of Engineering Designers
AMIE(Ind)	Associate Member, Institution of Engineers, India
AMIERE	Associate Member, Institution of Electronic and Radio Engineers
AMIH	Associate Member, Institute of Housing
AMIMinE	Associate Member, Institution of Mining Engineers
AMIMM	Associate Member, Institution of Mining and Metallurgy
AMInstBE	Associate Member, Institution of British Engineers
AMInstR	Associate Member, Institute of Refrigeration
AMInstTA	Associate Member, Institute of Traffic Adminstration
AMINucE	Associate Member, Institution of Nuclear Engineers
AMIStructE	Associate Member, Institution of Structural Engineers
AMN	Ahli Mangku Negara (Malaysia)
AMRINA	Associate Member, Royal Institution of Naval Architects
ANA	Associate National Academician (America)
ANECInst	Associate, NE Coast Institution of Engineers and Shipbuilders
AO	Officer of the Order of Australia
APMI	Associate, Pensions Management Institute
APsSI	Associate, Psychological Society of Ireland
ARA	Associate, Royal Academy
ARACI	Associate, Royal Australian Chemical Institute
ARAD	Associate, Royal Academy of Dancing
ARAeS	Associate, Royal Aeronautical Society
ARAM	Associate, Royal Academy of Music
ARAS	Associate, Royal Astronomical Society
ARBA	Associate, Royal Society of British Artists
ARBS	Associate, Royal Society of British Sculptors
ARCA	Associate, Royal College of Art; Associate, Royal Canadian Academy
ARCamA	Associate, Royal Cambrian Academy of Art
ARCM	Associate, Royal College of Music
ARCO	Associate, Royal College of Organists
ARCO(CHM)	Associate, Royal College of Organists with Diploma in Choir Training
ARCPsych	Associate Member, Royal College of Psychiatrists
ARCS	Associate, Royal College of Science
ARCST	Associate, Royal College of Science and Technology (Glasgow)
ARCVS	Associate, Royal College of Veterinary Surgeons
ARE	Associate, Royal Society of Painter-Etchers and Engravers
ARIAS	Associate, Royal Incorporation of Architects in Scotland

ARICS	Professional Associate, Royal Institution of Chartered Surveyors
ARINA	Associate, Royal Institution of Naval Architects
ARMS	Associate, Royal Society of Miniature Painters
ARPS	Associate, Royal Photographic Society
ARRC	Associate, Royal Red Cross
ARSA	Associate, Royal Scottish Academy
ARSCM	Associate, Royal School of Church Music
ARSM	Associate, Royal School of Mines
ARVIA	Associate, Royal Victoria Institute of Architects
ARWA	Associate, Royal West of England Academy
ARWS	Associate, Royal Society of Painters in Water-Colours
ASA	Associate Member, Society of Actuaries; Associate of Society of Actuaries (US)
ASAA	Associate, Society of Incorporated Accountants and Auditors
ASAM	Associate, Society of Art Masters
ASCA	Associate, Society of Company and Commercial Accountants
ASIAD	Associate, Society of Industrial Artists and Designers
ASIA(Ed)	Associate, Society of Industrial Artists (Education)
AssocISI	Associate, Iron and Steel Institute
AssocMIAeE	Associate Member, Institution of Aeronautical Engineers
AssocRINA	Associate, Royal Institution of Naval Architects
ATCL	Associate, Trinity College of Music, London
ATD	Art Teacher's Diploma
ATI	Associate, Textile Institute
ATII	Associate Member, Institute of Taxation
AVCM	Associate, Victoria College of Music
aws	Graduate of Air Warfare Course

B

BA	Bachelor of Arts
BAO	Bachelor of Art of Obstetrics
BAppSc(MT)	Bachelor of Applied Science (Medical Technology)
Bart or **Bt**	Baronet
BAS	Bachelor in Agricultural Science
BASc	Bachelor of Applied Science
BBA	Bachelor of Business Administration
BBM	Bintang Bakti Masharakat (Public Service Star) (Singapore)
BBS	Bachelor of Business Studies
BCE	Bachelor of Civil Engineering
BCh or **BChir**	Bachelor of Surgery

BCL	Bachelor of Civil Law
BCom or **BComm**	Bachelor of Commerce
BComSc	Bachelor of Commercial Science
BD	Bachelor of Divinity
BDS	Bachelor of Dental Surgery
BDSc	Bachelor of Dental Science
BE	Bachelor of Engineering
BE&A	Bachelor of Engineering and Architecture (Malta)
BEc	Bachelor of Economics
BEd	Bachelor of Education
BEE	Bachelor of Electrical Engineering
BEM	British Empire Medal
BJ	Bachelor of Journalism
BL	Bachelor of Law
BLE	Bachelor of Land Economy
BLitt	Bachelor of Letters
BM	Bachelor of Medicine
BMet	Bachelor of Metallurgy
BPharm	Bachelor of Pharmacy
BS	Bachelor of Surgery; Bachelor of Science
BSA	Bachelor of Scientific Agriculture
BSc	Bachelor of Science
BScA	Bachelor of Science in Agriculture
BSc(Dent)	Bachelor of Science in Dentistry
BSE	Bachelor of Science in Engineering (US)
BSocSc	Bachelor of Social Science
BST	Bachelor of Sacred Theology
BT	Bachelor of Teaching
Bt	Baronet
BTh	Bachelor of Theology
Btss	Baronetess
BVMS	Bachelor of Veterinary Medicine and Surgery

C

CA	Chartered Accountant (Scotland and Canada)
CAAV	Central Association of Agricultural Valuers; also Member of the Association
CB	Companion of the Order of the Bath
CBE	Commander of the Order of the British Empire
CBIM	Companion, British Institute of Management
CC	Companion of the Order of Canada
CCH	Cacique's Crown of Honour, Order of Service of Guyana
CChem	Chartered Chemist

CD	Canadian Forces Decoration; Commander of the Order of Distinction (Jamaica)
CDipAF	Certified Diploma in Accounting and Finance
CEng	Chartered Engineer
CF	Chaplain to the Forces
CFR	Commander of the Order of the Federal Republic of Nigeria
CGA	Community of the Glorious Ascension
CGH	Order of the Golden Heart of Kenya (lst class)
CGIA	Insignia Award of City and Guilds of London Institute
CGM	Conspicuous Gallantry Medal
CH	Companion of Honour
CHB	Companion of Honour of Barbados
ChB	Bachelor of Surgery
CHM	Chevalier of Honour and Merit (Haiti)
ChM	Master of Surgery
ChStJ	Chaplain of the Most Venerable Order of the Hospital of St John of Jerusalem
CIAgrE	Companion, Institution of Agricultural Engineers
CIAL	Corresponding Member of the International Institute of Arts and Letters
CIE	Companion of the Order of the Indian Empire
CIGasE	Companion, Institution of Gas Engineers
CIMarE	Companion, Institute of Marine Engineers
CIMGTechE	Companion, Institution of Mechanical and General Technician Engineers
CIPM	Companion, Institute of Personnel Management
CJM	Congregation of Jesus and Mary (Eudist Fathers)
CLit	Companion of Literature (Royal Society of Literature Award)
CLJ	Commander, Order of St Lazarus of Jerusalem
CM	Member of the Order of Canada; Congregation of the Mission (Vincentians); Master in Surgery; Certificated Master
CMA	Cost and Management Accountant (NZ)
CMG	Companion of the Order of St Michael and St George
CMLJ	Commander of Merit, Order of St Lazarus of Jerusalem
CMM	Commander, Order of Military Merit (Canada)
CMT	Chaconia Medal of Trinidad
CompAMEME	Companion, Association of Mining Electrical and Mechanical Engineers
CompIERE	Companion, Institution of Electronic and Radio Engineers
CompIWES	Companion, Institution of Water Engineers and Scientists
CompTI	Companion of the Textile Institute
CON	Commander, Order of the Niger
CPA	Chartered Patent Agent

CPM	Colonial Police Medal
CQSW	Certificate of Qualification in Social Work
CR	Community of the Resurrection
CRAeS	Companion, Royal Aeronautical Society
CRCP(C)	Certificant, Royal College of Physicians of Canada
CRNCM	Companion, Royal Northern College of Music
CSB	Bachelor of Christian Science
CSC	Conspicuous Service Cross; Congregation of the Holy Cross
CSD	Cooperative Secretaries Diploma
CSG	Companion of the Order of the Star of Ghana
CSI	Companion of the Order of the Star of India
CSS	Companion of the Star of Sarawak
CSSp	Holy Ghost Father
CSSR	Congregation of the Most Holy Redeemer (Redemptorist Order)
CStJ	Commander of the Most Venerable Order of the Hospital of St John of Jerusalem
CText	Chartered Textile Technologist
CV	Cross of Valour (Canada)
CVO	Commander of the Royal Victorian Order

D

DA	Diploma in Anaesthesia; Diploma in Art
DAgr	Doctor of Agriculture
DAppSc	Doctor of Applied Science
DASc	Doctor in Agricultural Sciences
DBA	Doctor of Business Administration
DBE	Dame Commander Order of the British Empire
DCAe	Diploma of College of Aeronautics
DCB	Dame Commander of the Order of the Bath
DCh	Doctor of Surgery
DCH	Diploma in Child Health
DCL	Doctor of Civil Law
DCM	Distinguished Conduct Medal
DCMG	Dame Commander of the Order of St Michael and St George
DCMHE	Diploma of Contents and Methods in Health Education
DCnL	Doctor of Canon Law
DCP	Diploma in Clinical Pathology; Diploma in Conservation of Paintings
DCS	Doctor of Commercial Sciences
DCT	Doctor of Christian Theology
DCVO	Dame Commander of Royal Victorian Order

DD	Doctor of Divinity
DDO	Diploma in Dental Orthopaedics
DDS	Doctor of Dental Surgery
DDSc	Doctor of Dental Science
DE	Doctor of Engineering
DEconSc	Doctor of Economic Science
DEd	Doctor of Education
DEng	Doctor of Engineering
DenM	Docteur en Médicine
DèsL	Docteur ès lettres
DèsS	Docteur ès sciences
DesRCA	Designer of the Royal College of Art
DFA	Doctor of Fine Arts
DFC	Distinguished Flying Cross
DFH	Diploma of Faraday House
DFM	Distinguished Flying Medal
DGS	Diploma in Graduate Studies
DGU	Doctor of Griffith University
DH	Doctor of Humanities
Dhc	Doctor *honoris causa*
DHL	Doctor of Humane Letters; Doctor of Hebrew Literature
DHMSA	Diploma in the History of Medicine (Society of Apothecaries)
DIC	Diploma of the Imperial College
DIH	Diploma in Industrial Health
DIMP	Darjah Indera Mahkota Pahang
DipAD	Diploma in Art and Design
DipAe	Diploma in Aeronautics
DipBA	Diploma in Business Administration
DipBS	Diploma in Fine Art, Byam Shaw School
DipCAM	Diploma in Communications, Advertising and Marketing of CAM Foundation
DipCC	Diploma of the Central College
DipCD	Diploma in Civic Design
DipCE	Diploma in Civil Engineering
DipEcon	Diploma in Economics
DipEd	Diploma in Education
DipESL	Diploma in English as a Second Language
DipEth	Diploma in Ethnology
DipFE	Diploma in Further Education
DipGSM	Diploma in Music, Guildhall School of Music and Drama
DipLA	Diploma in Landscape Architecture
DipLib	Diploma of Librarianship
DipM	Diploma in Marketing
DipTA	Diploma in Tropical Agriculture
DipT&CP	Diploma in Town and Country Planning

DipTP	Diploma in Town Planning
DipTPT	Diploma in Theory and Practice of Teaching
DistTP	Distinction in Town Planning
DJur	*Doctor Juris*
DK	Most Esteemed Family Order (Brunei)
DL	Deputy Lieutenant
DLC	Diploma Loughborough College
DLES	Doctor of Letters in Economic Studies
DLitt or **DLit**	Doctor of Literature; Doctor of Letters
DLJ	Dame of Grace, Order of St Lazarus of Jerusalem
DLO	Diploma in Laryngology and Otology
DM	Doctor of Medicine
DMA	Diploma in Municipal Administration
DMD	Doctor of Medical Dentistry (Australia)
DMet	Doctor of Metallurgy
DMin	Doctor of Ministry
DMJ	Diploma in Medical Jurisprudence
DMR	Diploma in Medical Radiology
DMRD	Diploma in Medical Radiological Diagnosis
DMRE	Diploma in Medical Radiology and Electrology
DMRT	Diploma in Medical Radio-Therapy
DMS	Decoration for Meritorious Service (South Africa); Diploma in Management Studies
DMus	Doctor of Music
DO	Diploma in Ophthalmology
DObstRCOG	Diploma Royal College of Obstetricians and Gynaecologists
DocEng	Doctor of Engineering
DOL	Doctor of Oriental Learning
DOMS	Diploma in Ophthalmic Medicine and Surgery
DPA	Diploma in Public Administration
DPD	Diploma in Public Dentistry
DPEc	Doctor of Political Economy
DPed	Doctor of Pedagogy
DPH	Diploma in Public Health
DPh or **DPhil**	Doctor of Philosophy
DPLG	Diplômé par le Gouvernement
DPM	Diploma in Psychological Medicine
DPS	Doctor of Public Service
DRC	Diploma of Royal College of Science and Technology, Glasgow
DRD	Diploma in Restorative Dentistry
Dr ing	Doctor of Engineering
Dr jur	Doctor of Laws
DrXcPol	Doctor Xconomiz Politicz

DRSAMD	Diploma of the Royal Scottish Academy of Music and Drama
DSA	Diploma in Social Administration
DSC	Distinguished Service Cross
DSc	Doctor of Science
DScA	Docteur en sciences agricoles
DSCHE	Diploma of the Scottish Council for Health Education
DScMil	Doctor of Military Science
DSLJ	Dato Seri Laila Jasa Brunei
DSM	Distinguished Service Medal
DSNB	Dato Setia Negara Brunei
DSO	Companion of the Distinguished Service Order
DSocSc	Doctor of Social Science
DSP	Docteur en sciences politiques (Montreal)
DSS	Doctor of Sacred Scripture
DSSc	Doctor of Social Science (USA)
DStJ	Dame of Justice, Most Venerable Order of the Hospital of St John of Jerusalem; Dame of Grace, Most Venerable Order of the Hospital of St John of Jerusalem
DTA	Diploma in Tropical Agriculture
DTD	Dekoratie voor Trouwe Dienst (Decoration for Devoted Service)
DTech	Doctor of Technology
DTH	Diploma in Tropical Hygiene
DTheol	Doctor of Theology
DThPT	Diploma in Theory and Practice of Teaching
DTM&H	Diploma in Tropical Medicine and Hygiene
DU	Doctor of the University
DUniv	Doctor of the University
DUP	Docteur de l'Université de Paris
DVH	Diploma in Veterinary Hygiene
DVM	Doctor of Veterinary Medicine
DVMS	Doctor of Veterinary Medicine and Surgery
DVR	Diploma in Veterinary Radiology
DVSc	Doctor of Veterinary Science
DVSM	Diploma in Veterinary State Medicine

E

EC	Etoile du Courage (Canada)
ED	Efficiency Decoration; Doctor of Engineering (US)
EdB	Bachelor of Education
EdD	Doctor of Education

EM	Edward Medal
ERD	Emergency Reserve Decoration (Army)

F

FAA	Fellow, Australian Academy of Science
FAAAS	Fellow, American Association for the Advancement of Science
FACC	Fellow, American College of Cardiology
FACCP	Fellow, American College of Chest Physicians
FACD	Fellow, American College of Dentistry
FACE	Fellow, Australian College of Education
FACOG	Fellow, American College of Obstetricians and Gynaecologists
FACP	Fellow, American College of Physicians
FACR	Fellow, American College of Radiology
FACS	Fellow, American College of Surgeons
FACVT	Fellow, American College of Veterinary Toxicology
FAGO	Fellowship in Australia in Obstetrics and Gynaecology
FAGS	Fellow, American Geographical Society
FAHA	Fellow, Australian Academy of the Humanities
FAIA	Fellow, American Institute of Architects
FAIAA	Fellow, American Institute of Aeronautics and Astronautics
FAIAS	Fellow, Australian Institute of Agricultural Science
FAIEx	Fellow, Australian Institute of Export
FAIFST	Fellow, Australian Institute of Food Science and Technology
FAIM	Fellow, Australian Institute of Management
FAIP	Fellow, Australian Institute of Physics
FAMS	Fellow, Ancient Monuments Society
FAPA	Fellow, American Psychiatric Association
FAPHA	Fellow, American Public Health Association
FAPS	Fellow, American Phytopathological Society
FArborA	Fellow, Arboricultural Association
FAS	Fellow, Antiquarian Society; Fellow, Nigerian Academy of Science
FASA	Fellow, Australian Society of Accountants
FASc	Fellow, Indian Academy of Sciences
FASCE	Fellow, American Society of Civil Engineers
FASSA	Fellow, Academy of the Social Sciences in Australia
FBA	Fellow, British Academy
FBCS	Fellow, British Computer Society
FBHI	Fellow, British Horological Institute
FBHS	Fellow, British Horse Society

FBIA	Fellow, Bankers' Institute of Australasia
FBIM	Fellow, British Institute of Management
FBINZ	Fellow, Bankers' Institute of New Zealand
FBIS	Fellow, British Interplanetary Society
FBKSTS	Fellow, British Kinematograph, Sound and Television Society
FBOA	Fellow, British Optical Association
FBOU	Fellow, British Ornithologists' Union
FBPsS	Fellow, British Psychological Society
FBSM	Fellow, Birmingham School of Music
FCA	Fellow, Institute of Chartered Accountants; Fellow, Institute of Chartered Accountants in Australia
FCAI	Fellow, New Zealand Institute of Cost Accountants
FCAM	Fellow, CAM Foundation
FCASI	Fellow, Canadian Aeronautics and Space Institute
FCBSI	Fellow, Chartered Building Societies Institute
FCCA	Fellow, Association of Certified Accountants
FCCEA	Fellow, Commonwealth Council for Educational Administration
FCCS	Fellow, Corporation of Secretaries (*formerly* of Certified Secretaries)
FCFI	Fellow, Clothing and Footwear Institute
FCGI	Fellow, City and Guilds of London Institute
FCH	Fellow, Coopers Hill College
FChS	Fellow, Society of Chiropodists
FCI	Fellow, Institute of Commerce
FCIA	Fellow, Corporation of Insurance Agents
FCIArb	Fellow, Chartered Institute of Arbitrators
FCIB	Fellow, Corporation of Insurance Brokers
FCIBS	Fellow, Chartered Institution of Building Services
FCIC	Fellow, Chemical Institute of Canada
FCII	Fellow, Chartered Insurance Institute
FCIOB	Fellow, Chartered Institute of Building
FCIS	Fellow, Institute of Chartered Secretaries and Administrators (*formerly* Chartered Institute of Secretaries)
FCIT	Fellow, Chartered Institute of Transport
FCMA	Fellow, Institute of Cost and Management Accountants
FCOG(SA)	Fellow, South African College of Obstetrics and Gynaecology
FCP	Fellow, College of Preceptors
FCPS	Fellow, College of Physicians and Surgeons
FCP(SoAf)	Fellow, College of Physicians, South Africa
FCPSO(SoAf)	Fellow, College of Physicians and Surgeons and Obstetricians, South Africa
FCSP	Fellow, Chartered Society of Physiotherapy

FCSSA, FCS(SoAf)	Fellow, College of Surgeons, South Africa
FCST	Fellow, College of Speech Therapists
FCT	Fellow, Association of Corporate Treasurers
FCTB	Fellow, College of Teachers of the Blind
FDS	Fellow in Dental Surgery
FDSRCPS Glas	Fellow in Dental Surgery, Royal College of Physicians and Surgeons of Glasgow
FDSRCS	Fellow in Dental Surgery, Royal College of Surgeons of England
FDSRCSE	Fellow in Dental Surgery, Royal College of Surgeons of Edinburgh
FEIS	Fellow, Educational Institute of Scotland
FEng	Fellow, Fellowship of Engineering
FES	Fellow, Entomological Society; Fellow, Ethnological Society
FFA	Fellow, Faculty of Actuaries (in Scotland)
FFARACS	Fellow, Faculty of Anaesthetists, Royal Australian College of Surgeons
FFARCS	Fellow, Faculty of Anaesthetists, Royal College of Surgeons of England
FFARCSI	Fellow, Faculty of Anaesthetists, Royal College of Surgeons in Ireland
FFAS	Fellow, Faculty of Architects and Surveyors, London
FFB	Fellow, Faculty of Building
FFCM	Fellow, Faculty of Community Medicine
FFDRCSI	Fellow, Faculty of Dentistry, Royal College of Surgeons in Ireland
FFHom	Fellow, Faculty of Homeopathy
FFOM	Fellow, Faculty of Occupational Medicine
FFPath, RCPI	Fellow, Faculty of Pathologists of the Royal College of Physicians of Ireland
FGA	Fellow, Gemmological Association
FGGE	Fellow, Guild of Glass Engineers
FGI	Fellow, Institute of Certificated Grocers
FGS	Fellow, Geological Society
FGSM	Fellow, Guildhall School of Music and Drama
FGSM(MT)	Fellow, Guildhall School of Music and Drama (Music Therapy)
FHA	Fellow, Institute of Health Service Administrators (*formerly* Hospital Administrators)
FHAS	Fellow, Highland and Agricultural Society of Scotland
FHCIMA	Fellow, Hotel Catering and Institutional Management Association
FHFS	Fellow, Human Factors Society
FHKIE	Fellow, Hong Kong Institution of Engineers
FHS	Fellow, Heraldry Society

FH-WC	Fellow, Heriot-Watt College (now University), Edinburgh
FIA	Fellow, Institute of Actuaries
FIAA	Fellow, Institute of Actuaries of Australia
FIAAS	Fellow, Institute of Australian Agricultural Science
FIAA&S	Fellow, Incorporated Association of Architects and Surveyors
FIAgrE	Fellow, Institution of Agricultural Engineers
FIAI	Fellow, Institute of Industrial and Commercial Accountants
FIAL	Fellow, International Institute of Arts and Letters
FIAM	Fellow, Institute of Administrative Management; Fellow, International Academy of Management
FIAP	Fellow, Institution of Analysts and Programmers
FIArbA	Fellow, Institute of Arbitrators of Australia
FIAWS	Fellow, International Academy of Wood Sciences
FIB	Fellow, Institute of Bankers
FIBD	Fellow, Institute of British Decorators
FIBP	Fellow, Institute of British Photographers
FIBiol	Fellow, Institute of Biology
FIBScot	Fellow, Institute of Bankers in Scotland
FICAI	Fellow, Institute of Chartered Accountants in Ireland
FICD	Fellow, Institute of Civil Defence; Fellow, Indian College of Dentists
FICE	Fellow, Institution of Civil Engineers
FICeram	Fellow, Institute of Ceramics
FICFor	Fellow, Institute of Chartered Foresters
FIChemE	Fellow, Institution of Chemical Engineers
FICI	Fellow, Institute of Chemistry of Ireland
FICorrST	Fellow, Institution of Corrosion Science and Technology
FICS	Fellow, Institute of Chartered Shipbrokers; Fellow, International College of Surgeons
FICW	Fellow, Institute of Clerks of Works of Great Britain
FIDCA	Fellow, Industrial Design Council of Australia
FIE(Aust)	Fellow, Institution of Engineers, Australia
FIED	Fellow, Institution of Engineering Designers
FIEE	Fellow, Institution of Electrical Engineers
FIEEE	Fellow, Institute of Electrical and Electronics Engineers (NY)
FIERE	Fellow, Institution of Electronic and Radio Engineers
FIExpE	Fellow, Institute of Explosives Engineers
FIFE	Fellow, Institution of Fire Engineers
FIFM	Fellow, Institute of Fisheries Management
FIFST	Fellow, Institute of Food Science and Technology
FIGasE	Fellow, Institution of Gas Engineers
FIGCM	Fellow, Incorporated Guild of Church Musicians
FIGD	Fellow, Institute of Grocery Distribution

FIGO	International Federation of Gynaecology and Obstetrics
FIH	Fellow, Institute of Housing; Fellow, Institute of the Horse
FIHE	Fellow, Institute of Health Education
FIHospE	Fellow, Institute of Hospital Engineering
FIIC	Fellow, International Institute for Conservation of Historic and Artistic Works
FIIM	Fellow, Institution of Industrial Managers
FIInfSc	Fellow, Institute of Information Scientists
FIInst	Fellow, Imperial Institute
FIIP	Fellow, Institute of Incorporated Photographers
FIIPE	Fellow, Indian Institution of Production Engineers
FIL	Fellow, Institute of Linguists
Fil.Hed.	Filosofie Hedersdoktor
FIllumES	Fellow, Illuminating Engineering Society
FIM	Fellow, Institution of Metallurgists
FIMA	Fellow, Institute of Mathematics and its Applications
FIMarE	Fellow, Institute of Marine Engineers
FIMC	Fellow, Institute of Management Consultants
FIMechE	Fellow, Institution of Mechanical Engineers
FIMGTechE	Fellow, Institution of Mechanical and General Technician Engineers
FIMH	Fellow, Institute of Materials Handling; Fellow, Institute of Military History
FIMI	Fellow, Institute of the Motor Industry
FIMinE	Fellow, Institution of Mining Engineers
FIMIT	Fellow, Institute of Musical Instrument Technology
FIMLS	Fellow, Institute of Medical Laboratory Sciences
FIMM	Fellow, Institute of Mining and Metallurgy
FIMS	Fellow, Institute of Mathematical Statistics
FIMunE	Fellow, Institution of Municipal Engineers
FInstAM	Fellow, Institute of Administrative Management
FInstB	Fellow, Institution of Buyers
FInstD	Fellow, Institute of Directors
FInstE	Fellow, Institute of Energy
FInstFF	Fellow, Institute of Freight Forwarders Ltd
FInstHE	Fellow, Institution of Highways Engineers
FInstLEx	Fellow, Institute of Legal Executives
FInstM	Fellow, Institute of Meat; Fellow, Institute of Marketing
FInstMC	Fellow, Institute of Measurement and Control
FInstP	Fellow, Institute of Physics
FInstPet	Fellow, Institute of Petroleum
FInstPI	Fellow, Institute of Patentees and Inventors
FInstPS	Fellow, Institute of Purchasing and Supply
FInstSMM	Fellow, Institute of Sales and Marketing Management
FInstWPC	Fellow, Institute of Water Pollution Control
FINucE	Fellow, Institution of Nuclear Engineers

FIOA	Fellow, Institute of Acoustics
FIOP	Fellow, Institute of Printing
FIPA	Fellow, Institute of Practitioners in Advertising
FIPDM	Fellow, Institute of Physical Distribution Management
FIPENZ	Fellow, Institution of Professional Engineers, New Zealand
FIPHE	Fellow, Institution of Public Health Engineers
FIPM	Fellow, Institute of Personnel Management
FIPR	Fellow, Institute of Public Relations
FIProdE	Fellow, Institution of Production Engineers
FIQ	Fellow, Institute of Quarrying
FIQA	Fellow, Institute of Quality Assurance
FIQPS	Fellow, Institute of Qualified Private Secretaries
FIQS	Fellow, Institute of Quantity Surveyors
FIRA(Ind)	Fellow, Institute of Railway Auditors and Accountants (India)
FIREE(Aust)	Fellow, Institution of Radio and Electronics Engineers (Australia)
FIRTE	Fellow, Institute of Road Transport Engineers
FIS	Fellow, Institute of Statisticians
FISA	Fellow, Incorporated Secretaries' Association
FISE	Fellow, Institution of Sales Engineers; Fellow, Institution of Sanitary Engineers
FIST	Fellow, Institute of Science Technology
FISTC	Fellow, Institute of Scientific and Technical Communicators
FIStructE	Fellow, Institution of Structural Engineers
FISW	Fellow, Institute of Social Work
FITD	Fellow, Institute of Training and Development
FITE	Fellow, Institution of Electrical and Electronics Technician Engineers
FIWES	Fellow, Institution of Water Engineers and Scientists
FIWPC	Fellow, Institute of Water Pollution Control
FIWSc	Fellow, Institute of Wood Science
FJI	Fellow, Institute of Journalists
FKC	Fellow, King's College London
FKCHMS	Fellow, King's College Hospital Medical School
FLA	Fellow, Library Association
FLAI	Fellow, Library Association of Ireland
FLCM	Fellow, London College of Music
FLHS	Fellow, London Historical Society
FLI	Fellow, Landscape Institute
FLIA	Fellow, Life Insurance Association
FLS	Fellow, Linnean Society
FMA	Fellow, Museums Association

FMANZ	Fellow, Medical Association of New Zealand
FMS	Fellow, Institute of Management Services
FMSA	Fellow, Mineralogical Society of America
FNA	Fellow, Indian National Science Academy
FNECInst	Fellow, North East Coast Institution of Engineers and Shipbuilders
FNI	Fellow, Nautical Institute
FNZIA	Fellow, New Zealand Institute of Architects
FNZIAS	Fellow, New Zealand Institute of Agricultural Science
FNZIC	Fellow, New Zealand Institute of Chemistry
FNZIE	Fellow, New Zealand Institution of Engineers
FNZIM	Fellow, New Zealand Institute of Management
FPEA	Fellow, Physical Education Association
FPhS	Fellow, Philosophical Society of England
FPI	Fellow, Plastics Institute (*now see* FPRI)
FPMI	Fellow, Pensions Management Institute
FPRI	Fellow, Plastics and Rubber Institute
FPS	Fellow, Pharmaceutical Society
FPhysS	Fellow, Physical Society
FRACDS	Fellow, Royal Australian College of Dental Surgeons
FRACGP	Fellow, Royal Australian College of General Practitioners
FRACI	Fellow, Royal Australian Chemical Institute
FRACMA	Fellow, Royal Australian College of Medical Administrators
FRACO	Fellow, Royal Australian College of Ophthalmologists
FRACOG	Fellow, Royal Australian College of Obstetricians and Gynaecologists
FRACP	Fellow, Royal Australasian College of Physicians
FRACR	Fellow, Royal Australasian College of Radiologists
FRACS	Fellow, Royal Australasian College of Surgeons
FRAD	Fellow, Royal Academy of Dancing
FRAeS	Fellow, Royal Aeronautical Society
FRAgS	Fellow, Royal Agricultural Societies (ie of England, Scotland and Wales)
FRAHS	Fellow, Royal Australian Historical Society
FRAI	Fellow, Royal Anthropological Institute
FRAIA	Fellow, Royal Australian Institute of Architects
FRAIB	Fellow, Royal Australian Institute of Building
FRAIC	Fellow, Royal Architectural Institute of Canada
FRAM	Fellow, Royal Academy of Music
FRAME	Fund for the Replacement of Animals in Medical Experiments
FRANZCP	Fellow, Royal Australian and New Zealand College of Psychiatrists
FRAPI	Fellow, Royal Australian Planning Institute

FRAS	Fellow, Royal Astronomical Society; Fellow, Royal Asiatic Society
FRASB	Fellow, Royal Asiatic Society of Bengal
FRASE	Fellow, Royal Agricultural Society of England
FRBS	Fellow, Royal Society of British Sculptors; Fellow, Royal Botanic Society
FRCGP	Fellow, Royal College of General Practitioners
FRCM	Fellow, Royal College of Music
FRCN	Fellow, Royal College of Nursing
FRCO	Fellow, Royal College of Organists
FRCO(CHM)	Fellow, Royal College of Organists with Diploma in Choir Training
FRCOG	Fellow, Royal College of Obstetricians and Gynaecologists
FRCP	Fellow, Royal College of Physicians, London
FRCPA	Fellow, Royal College of Pathologists of Australasia
FRCP&S (Canada)	Fellow, Royal College of Physicians and Surgeons of Canada
FRCPath	Fellow, Royal College of Pathologists
FRCP(C)	Fellow, Royal College of Physicians of Canada
FRCPE and **FRCPEd**	Fellow, Royal College of Physicians, Edinburgh
FRCPGlas	Fellow, Royal College of Physicians and Surgeons of Glasgow
FRCPI	Fellow, Royal College of Physicians of Ireland
FRCPsych	Fellow, Royal College of Psychiatrists
FRCR	Fellow, Royal College of Radiologists
FRCS	Fellow, Royal College of Surgeons of England
FRCSE and **FRCSEd**	Fellow, Royal College of Surgeons of Edinburgh
FRCSGlas	Fellow, Royal College of Physicians and Surgeons of Glasgow
FRCSI	Fellow, Royal College of Surgeons in Ireland
FRCSoc	Fellow, Royal Commonwealth Society
FRCUS	Fellow, Royal College of University Surgeons (Denmark)
FRCVS	Fellow, Royal College of Veterinary Surgeons
FREconS	Fellow, Royal Economic Society
FREI	Fellow, Real Estate Institute (Australia)
FRES	Fellow, Royal Entomological Society of London
FRGS	Fellow, Royal Geographical Society
FRGSA	Fellow, Royal Geographical Society of Australasia
FRHistS	Fellow, Royal Historical Society
FRHS	Fellow, Royal Horticultural Society
FRIAS	Fellow, Royal Incorporation of Architects of Scotland
FRIBA	Fellow, Royal Institute of British Architects
FRICS	Fellow, Royal Institution of Chartered Surveyors
FRIH	Fellow, Royal Institute of Horticulture (NZ)
FRIN	Fellow, Royal Institute of Navigation
FRINA	Fellow, Royal Institution of Naval Architects

FRIPHH	Fellow, Royal Institute of Public Health and Hygiene
FRMCM	Fellow, Royal Manchester College of Music
FRMedSoc	Fellow, Royal Medical Society
FRMetS	Fellow, Royal Meteorological Society
FRMIA	Fellow, Retail Management Institute of Australia
FRMS	Fellow, Royal Microscopical Society
FRNCM	Fellow, Royal Northern College of Music
FRNS	Fellow, Royal Numismatic Society
FRPS	Fellow, Royal Photographic Society
FRPSL	Fellow, Royal Philatelic Society, London
FRS	Fellow, Royal Society
FRSA	Fellow, Royal Society of Arts
FRSAI	Fellow, Royal Society of Antiquaries of Ireland
FRSAMD	Fellow, Royal Scottish Academy of Music and Drama
FRSC	Fellow, Royal Society of Canada; Fellow, Royal Society of Chemistry
FRSCM	Fellow, Royal School of Church Music
FRSE	Fellow, Royal Society of Edinburgh
FRSGS	Fellow, Royal Scottish Geographical Society
FRSH	Fellow, Royal Society for the Promotion of Health
FRSL	Fellow, Royal Society of Literature
FRSNZ	Fellow, Royal Society of New Zealand
FRSSAf	Fellow, Royal Society of South Africa
FRST	Fellow, Royal Society of Teachers
FRSTM&H	Fellow, Royal Society of Tropical Medicine and Hygiene
FRTPI	Fellow, Royal Town Planning Institute
FRTS	Fellow, Royal Television Society
FRVA	Fellow, Rating and Valuation Association
FRVC	Fellow, Royal Veterinary College
FRVIA	Fellow, Royal Victorian Institute of Architects
FRZSScot	Fellow, Royal Zoological Society of Scotland
FSA	Fellow, Society of Antiquaries
FSAA	Fellow, Society of Incorporated Accountants and Auditors
FSAE	Fellow, Society of Automotive Engineers
FSAIEE	Fellow, South African Institute of Electrical Engineers
FSAM	Fellow, Society of Art Masters
FSAScot	Fellow, Society of Antiquaries of Scotland
FSASM	Fellow, South Australian School of Mines
FSBI	Fellow, Savings Banks Institute
FSCA	Fellow, Society of Company and Commercial Accountants
FSDC	Fellow, Society of Dyers and Colourists
FSE	Fellow, Society of Engineers
FSG	Fellow, Society of Genealogists
FSGT	Fellow, Society of Glass Technology
FSIAD	Fellow, Society of Industrial Artists and Designers

FSLAET	Fellow, Society of Licensed Aircraft Engineers and Technologists
FSS	Fellow, Royal Statistical Society
FSTD	Fellow, Society of Typographic Designers
FSVA	Fellow, Incorporated Society of Valuers and Auctioneers
FTCD	Fellow, Trinity College, Dublin
FTCL	Fellow, Trinity College of Music, London
FTI	Fellow, Textile Institute
FTII	Fellow, Institute of Taxation
FTP	Fellow, Thames Polytechnic
FTS	Fellow, Australian Academy of Technological Sciences
FUMIST	Fellow, University of Manchester Institute of Science and Technology
FWA	Fellow, World Academy of Arts and Sciences
FWACP	Fellow, West African College of Physicians
FWeldI	Fellow, Welding Institute
FZS	Fellow, Zoological Society

G

GBE	Knight or Dame Grand Cross of the Order of the British Empire
GBSM	Graduate of Birmingham and Midland Institute School of Music
GC	George Cross
GCB	Knight or Dame Grand Cross of the Order of the Bath
GCFR	Grand Commander of the Order of the Federal Republic of Nigeria
GCIE	Knight Grand Commander of the Order of the Indian Empire
GCLJ	Grand Cross, St Lazarus of Jerusalem
GCM	Gold Crown of Merit (Barbados)
GCMG	Knight or Dame Grand Cross of the Order of St Michael and St George
GCON	Grand Cross, Order of the Niger
GCSG	Knight Grand Cross of the Order of St Gregory the Great
GCSI	Grand Commander of the Order of the Star of India
GCSJ	Knight Grand Cross of Justice, Order of St John of Jerusalem (Knights Hospitaller)
GCStJ	Bailiff or Dame Grand Cross of the Most Venerable Order of the Hospital of St John of Jerusalem
GCVO	Knight or Dame Grand Cross of the Royal Victorian Order
GGSM	Graduate in Music, Guildhall School of Music and Drama

GM	George Medal; Grand Medal (Ghana)
GRSM	Graduate of the Royal Schools of Music
GTCL	Graduate, Trinity College of Music

H

HBM	Humming Bird Gold Medal (Trinidad)
HDD	Higher Dental Diploma
HDipEd	Higher Diploma in Education
HH	Member, Hesketh Hubbard Art Society
HHD	Doctor of Humanities (US)
HJ	Hilal-e-Jurat (Pakistan)
HLD	Doctor of Humane Letters
HPk	Hilal-e-Pakistan
HQA	Hilal-i-Quaid-i-Azam (Pakistan)

I

ICD	*Iuris Canonici Doctor*
IPFA	Member or Associate, Chartered Institute of Public Finance and Accountancy
ISO	Imperial Service Order

J

JCB	*Juris Canonici* (or *Civilis*) *Baccalaureus* (Bachelor of Canon (or Civil) Law)
JCD	*Juris Canonici* (or *Civilis*) *Doctor* (Doctor of Canon (or Civil) Law)
JCL	*Juris Canonici* (or *Civilis*) *Licentiatus* (Licentiate in Canon (or Civil) Law)
JD	Doctor of Jurisprudence
JDipMA	Joint Diploma in Management Accounting Services
JMN	Johan Mangku Negara (Malaysia)
JP	Justice of the Peace
JSD	Doctor of Juristic Science
JSM	Johan Setia Mahkota (Malaysia)
JUD	*Juris Utriusque Doctor*, Doctor of Both Laws (Canon and Civil)

K

KBE	Knight Commander Order of the British Empire
KC	King's Counsel
KCB	Knight Commander of the Order of the Bath
KCHS	Knight Commander, Order of the Holy Sepulchre
KCIE	Knight Commander, Order of the Indian Empire
KCLJ	Knight Commander, Order of St Lazarus of Jerusalem
KCMG	Knight Commander, Order of St Michael and St George
KCSA	Knight Commander, Military Order of the Collar of St Agatha of Paterna
KCSG	Knight Commander, Order of St Gregory the Great
KCSI	Knight Commander, Order of the Star of India
KCSS	Knight Commander, Order of St Silvester
KCVO	Knight Commander of the Royal Victorian Order
KG	Knight of the Order of the Garter
KHC	Hon. Chaplain to the King
KHDS	Hon. Dental Surgeon to the King
KHNS	Hon. Nursing Sister to the King
KHP	Hon. Physician to the King
KHS	Hon. Surgeon to the King; Knight of the Holy Sepulchre
KLJ	Knight, St Lazarus of Jerusalem
KPM	King's Police Medal
KSC	Knight of St Columba
KSG	Knight of the Order of St Gregory the Great
KSJ	Knight of the Order of St John of Jerusalem (Knights Hospitaller)
KSS	Knight of St Silvester
KStJ	Knight of the Most Venerable Order of the Hospital of St John of Jerusalem
KT	Knight of the Order of the Thistle

L

LC	Cross of Leo
LCh	Licentiate in Surgery
LCP	Licentiate, College of Preceptors
LCST	Licentiate, College of Speech Therapists
LDiv	Licentiate in Divinity
LDS	Licentiate in Dental Surgery
LwesL	Licencié ès lettres
LGSM	Licentiate, Guildhall School of Music and Drama
LHD	Literarum Humaniorum Doctor (Doctor of Literature)
LicMed	Licentiate in Medicine
LIOB	Licentiate, Institute of Building

LitD or **LittD**	Doctor of Literature; Doctor of Letters
LLB	Bachelor of Laws
LLCM	Licentiate, London College of Music
LLD	Doctor of Laws
LLL	Licentiate in Laws
LLM	Master of Laws
LM	Licentiate in Midwifery
LMCC	Licentiate, Medical Council of Canada
LMed	Licentiate in Medicine
LMSSA	Licentiate in Medicine and Surgery, Society of Apothecaries
LMRTPI	Legal Member, Royal Town Planning Institute
LRAD	Licentiate, Royal Academy of Dancing
LRAM	Licentiate, Royal Academy of Music
LRCP	Licentiate, Royal College of Physicians, London
LRCPE	Licentiate, Royal College of Physicians, Edinburgh
LRCPI	Licentiate, Royal College of Physicians of Ireland
LRCPSGlas	Licentiate, Royal College of Physicians and Surgeons of Glasgow
LRCS	Licentiate, Royal College of Surgeons of England
LRCSE	Licentiate, Royal College of Surgeons, Edinburgh
LRCSI	Licentiate, Royal College of Surgeons in Ireland
LSA	Licentiate, Society of Apothecaries; Licence in Agricultural Sciences
LT	Licentiate in Teaching
LTCL	Licentiate of Trinity College of Music, London
LTh	Licentiate in Theology

M

MA	Master of Arts
MAAT	Member, Association of Accounting Technicians
MACE	Member, Australian College of Education; Member, Association of Conference Executives
MACI	Member, American Concrete Institute
MACM	Member, Association of Computing Machines
MACS	Member, American Chemical Society
MAIAA	Member, American Institute of Aeronautics and Astronautics
MAICE	Member, American Institute of Consulting Engineers
MAIChE	Member, American Institute of Chemical Engineers
MAO	Master of Obstetric Art
MAOT	Member, Association of Occupational Therapists
MAOU	Member, American Ornithologists' Union
MAPsS	Member, Australian Psychological Society

MArch	Master of Architecture
MASAE	Member, American Society of Agricultural Engineers
MASCE	Member, American Society of Civil Engineers
MASME	Member, American Society of Mechanical Engineers
MAusIMM	Member, Australasian Institute of Mining and Metallurgy
MB	Medal of Bravery (Canada); Bachelor of Medicine
MBA	Master of Business Administration
MBASW	Member, British Association of Social Workers
MBCS	Member, British Computer Society
MBE	Member, Order of the British Empire
MBHI	Member, British Horological Institute
MBKSTS	Member, British Kinematograph, Sound and Television Society
MBOU	Member, British Ornithologists' Union
MC	Military Cross; Missionaries of Charity
MCAM	Member, CAM Foundation
MCB	Master in Clinical Biochemistry
MCBSI	Member, Chartered Building Societies Institute
MCD	Master of Civic Design
MCE	Master of Civil Engineering
MCFP	Member, College of Family Physicians (Canada)
MCh or **MChir**	Master in Surgery
MChE	Master of Chemical Engineering
MChemA	Master in Chemical Analysis
MChOrth	Master of Orthopaedic Surgery
MCIBS	Member, Chartered Institution of Building Services
MCIOB	Member, Chartered Institute of Building
M.CIRP	Member, International Institution for Production Engineering Research
MCIT	Member, Chartered Institute of Transport
MCL	Master in Civil Law
MCMES	Member, Civil and Mechanical Engineers' Society
MCom	Master of Commerce
MConsE	Member, Association of Consulting Engineers
MCP	Master of City Planning (US)
MCPS	Member, College of Physicians and Surgeons
MCSEE	Member, Canadian Society of Electrical Engineers
MCSP	Member, Chartered Society of Physiotherapy
MCST	Member, College of Speech Therapists
MCT	Member, Association of Corporate Treasurers
MD	Doctor of Medicine
MDes	Master of Design
MDS	Master of Dental Surgery
ME	Master of Engineering
MEC	Member of Executive Council

MEc	Master of Economics
MECI	Member, Institute of Employment Consultants
MEd	Master of Education
MEIC	Member, Engineering Institute of Canada
MEng	Master of Engineering
MEP	Member of the European Parliament
MFA	Master of Fine Arts
MFC	Mastership in Food Control
MFCM	Member, Faculty of Community Medicine
MFH	Master of Foxhounds
MFOM	Member, Faculty of Occupational Medicine
MGDS RCS	Member in General Dental Surgery, Royal College of Surgeons
MGI	Member, Institute of Certificated Grocers
MGO	Master of Gynaecology and Obstetrics
MHA	Member of House of Assembly
MHCIMA	Member, Hotel Catering and Institutional Management Association
MHK	Member of the House of Keys
MHR	Member of the House of Representatives
MIAeE	Member, Institute of Aeronautical Engineers
MIAgrE	Member, Institution of Agricultural Engineers
MIAM	Member, Institute of Administrative Management
MIBF	Member, Institute of British Foundrymen
MIBritE	Member, Institution of British Engineers
MIBS	Member, Institute of Bankers in Scotland
MICE	Member, Institution of Civil Engineers
MICEI	Member, Institution of Civil Engineers of Ireland
MICFor	Member, Institute of Chartered Foresters
MIChemE	Member, Institution of Chemical Engineers
MICorrST	Member, Institution of Corrosion Science and Technology
MICS	Member, Institute of Chartered Shipbrokers
MIDPM	Member, Institute of Data Processing Management
MIE(Aust)	Member, Institution of Engineers, Australia
MIED	Member, Institution of Engineering Designers
MIEE	Member, Institution of Electrical Engineers
MIEEE	Member, Institute of Electrical and Electronics Engineers (NY)
MIEI	Member, Institution of Engineering Inspection
MIE(Ind)	Member, Institution of Engineers, India
MIERE	Member, Institution of Electronic and Radio Engineers
MIES	Member, Institution of Engineers and Shipbuilders, Scotland
MIEx	Member, Institute of Export
MIExpE	Member, Institute of Explosives Engineers

MIFF	Member, Institute of Freight Forwarders
MIGasE	Member, Institution of Gas Engineers
MIGeol	Member, Institution of Geologists
MIH	Member, Institute of Housing
MIIM	Member, Institution of Industrial Managers
MIInfSc	Member, Institute of Information Sciences
MIL	Member, Institute of Linguists
MILGA	Member, Institute of Local Government Administrators
MILocoE	Member, Institution of Locomotive Engineers
MIM	Member, Institution of Metallurgists
MIMarE	Member, Institute of Marine Engineers
MIMC	Member, Institute of Management Consultants
MIMechE	Member, Institution of Mechanical Engineers
MIMGTechE	Member, Institution of Mechanical and General Technician Engineers
MIMI	Member, Institute of the Motor Industry
MIMinE	Member, Institution of Mining Engineers
MIMM	Member, Institution of Mining and Metallurgy
MIMunE	Member, Institution of Municipal Engineers
MInstAM	Member, Institute of Administrative Management
MInstBE	Member, Institution of British Engineers
MInstD	Member, Institute of Directors
MInstE	Member, Institute of Energy
MInstEnvSci	Member, Institute of Environmental Sciences
MInstGasE	Member, Institution of Gas Engineers
MInstHE	Member, Institution of Highway Engineers
MInstM	Member, Institute of Marketing
MInstMC	Member, Institute of Measurement and Control
MInstME	Member, Institution of Mining Engineers
MInstP	Member, Institute of Physics
MInstPet	Member, Institute of Petroleum
MInstPI	Member, Institute of Patentees and Inventors
MInstPkg	Member, Institute of Packaging
MInstPS	Member, Institute of Purchasing and Supply
MInstR	Member, Institute of Refrigeration
MInstRA	Member, Institute of Registered Architects
MInstT	Member, Institute of Transport
MInstTM	Member, Institute of Travel Managers in Industry and Commerce
MINucE	Member, Institution of Nuclear Engineers
MIPA	Member, Institute of Practitioners in Advertising
MIPM	Member, Institute of Personnel Management
MIPR	Member, Institute of Public Relations
MIProdE	Member, Institution of Production Engineers
MIQ	Member, Institute of Quarrying

MIREE(Aust)	Member, Institution of Radio and Electronics Engineers (Australia)
MIRT	Member, Institute of Reprographic Technicians
MIRTE	Member, Institute of Road Transport Engineers
MIS	Member, Institute of Statisticians
MIS(India)	Member, Institution of Surveyors of India
MIStructE	Member, Institution of Structural Engineers
MITA	Member, Industrial Transport Association
MITD	Member, Institute of Training and Development
MITE	Member, Institution of Electrical and Electronics Technician Engineers
MITT	Member, Institute of Travel and Tourism
MIWES	Member, Institution of Water Engineers and Scientists
MIWPC	Member, Institute of Water Pollution Control
MJI	Member, Institute of Journalists
MJur	*Magister Juris*
ML	Licentiate in Medicine; Master of Laws
MLA	Member of Legislative Assembly; Master in Landscape Architecture
MLC	Member of Legislative Council
MLitt	Master of Letters
MM	Military Medal
MME	Master of Mining Engineering
MMechE	Master of Mechanical Engineering
MMet	Master of Metallurgy
MMGI	Member, Mining, Geological and Metallurgical Institute of India
MMM	Member, Order of Military Merit (Canada)
MMS	Member, Institute of Management Services
MMSA	Master of Midwifery, Society of Apothecaries
MNAS	Member, National Academy of Sciences (US)
MNECInst	Member, North East Coast Institution of Engineers and Shipbuilders
MNI	Member, Nautical Institute
MNSE	Member, Nigerian Society of Engineers
MP	Member of Parliament
MPA	Master of Public Administration
MPH	Master of Public Health
MPP	Member, Provincial Parliament
MPS	Member, Pharmaceutical Society
MRAC	Member, Royal Agricultural College
MRACP	Member, Royal Australasian College of Physicians
MRACS	Member, Royal Australasian College of Surgeons
MRAeS	Member, Royal Aeronautical Society
MRAIC	Member, Royal Architectural Institute of Canada
MRAS	Member, Royal Asiatic Society

MRCGP	Member, Royal College of General Practitioners
MRCOG	Member, Royal College of Obstetricians and Gynaecologists
MRCP	Member, Royal College of Physicians, London
MRCPA	Member, Royal College of Pathologists of Australia
MRCPE	Member, Royal College of Physicians, Edinburgh
MRCPGlas	Member, Royal College of Physicians and Surgeons of Glasgow
MRCPI	Member, Royal College of Physicians of Ireland
MRCPsych	Member, Royal College of Psychiatrists
MRCS	Member, Royal College of Surgeons of England
MRCSE	Member, Royal College of Surgeons of Edinburgh
MRCSI	Member, Royal College of Surgeons in Ireland
MRCVS	Member, Royal College of Veterinary Surgeons
MRE	Master of Religious Education
MRI	Member, Royal Institution
MRIA	Member, Royal Irish Academy
MRIAI	Member, Royal Institute of the Architects of Ireland
MRIN	Member, Royal Institute of Navigation
MRINA	Member, Royal Institution of Naval Architects
MRSC	Member, Royal Society of Chemistry
MRSH	Member, Royal Society for the Promotion of Health
MRSL	Member, Order of the Republic of Sierra Leone
MRST	Member, Royal Society of Teachers
MRTPI	Member, Royal Town Planning Institute
MRUSI	Member, Royal United Service Institution
MRVA	Member, Rating and Valuation Association
MS	Master of Surgery; Master of Science (US)
MSA	Master of Science, Agriculture (US)
MSAE	Member, Society of Automotive Engineers (US)
MSAICE	Member, South African Institution of Civil Engineers
MSAInstMM	Member, South African Institute of Mining and Metallurgy
MSAutE	Member, Society of Automobile Engineers
MSC	Missionaries of the Sacred Heart
MSc	Master of Science
MScD	Master of Dental Science
MSE	Master of Science in Engineering (US)
MSIAD	Member, Society of Industrial Artists and Designers
MSINZ	Member, Surveyors' Institute of New Zealand
MSM	Meritorious Service Medal
MSocIS	Member, Société des Ingénieurs et Scientifiques de France
MSocSc	Master of Social Sciences
MSR	Member, Society of Radiographers
MSTD	Member, Society of Typographic Designers
MTAI	Member, Institute of Travel Agents

MTD	Midwife Teachers' Diploma
MTEFL	Master in the Teaching of English as a Foreign or Second Language
MTh	Master of Theology
MTS	Master of Theological Studies
MusB	Bachelor of Music
MusD	Doctor of Music
MusM	Master of Music
MVO	Member, Royal Victorian Order
MVSc	Master of Veterinary Science
MWeldI	Member, Welding Institute

N

NDA	National Diploma in Agriculture
NDD	National Diploma in Dairying; National Diploma in Design
NDH	National Diploma in Horticulture
NEAC	New English Art Club
NNOM	Nigerian National Order of Merit
NPk	Nishan-e-Pakistan
NRD	National Registered Designer
NSAIV	Distinguished Order of Shaheed Ali (Maldives)

O

OBE	Officer, Order of the British Empire
OC	Officer of the Order of Canada
OD	Officer of the Order of Distinction (Jamaica)
OE	Order of Excellence (Guyana)
OFM	Order of Friars Minor (Franciscans)
OFMCap	Order of Friars Minor Capuchin (Franciscans)
OFMConv	Order of Friars Minor Conventual (Franciscans)
OFR	Order of the Federal Republic of Nigeria
OJ	Order of Jamaica
OL	Officer of the Order of Leopold
OM	Order of Merit
OMI	Oblate of Mary Immaculate
OMM	Officer, Order of Military Merit (Canada)
ON	Order of the Nation (Jamaica)
OON	Officer of the Order of the Niger
OP	*Ordinis Praedicatorum*: of the Order of Preachers (Dominican); Observation Post
OR	Order of Rorima (Guyana)

ORSL	Order of the Republic of Sierra Leone
OSA	Order of St Augustine (Augustinian)
OSB	Order of St Benedict (Benedictine)
OSFC	Franciscan (Capuchin) Order
OStJ	Officer of the Most Venerable Order of the Hospital of St John of Jerusalem
OTL	Officer of the Order of Toussaint L'Ouverture (Haiti)

P

PAA	President, Australian Academy of Science
PAg	Professional Agronomist
PC	Privy Counsellor
PdD	Doctor of Pedagogy (US)
PEng	Registered Professional Engineer (Canada)
PH	Presidential Order of Honour (Botswana)
PhB	Bachelor of Philosophy
PhD	Doctor of Philosophy
PhL	Licentiate of Philosophy
PhM	Master of Philosophy (USA)
PhmB	Bachelor of Pharmacy
PJK	Pingkat Jasa Kebaktian (Malaysia)
PMN	Panglima Mangku Negara (Malaysia)
PMS	Presidential Order of Meritorious Service (Botswana); President, Miniature Society
PNBS	Panglima Negara Bintang Sarawak
POB	Presidential Order of Botswana
PPRA	Past President of the Royal Academy
PPRBA	Past President of the Royal Society of British Artists
PPRBS	Past President, Royal Society of British Sculptors
PPRE	Past President of the Royal Society of Painter-Etchers and Engravers
PPRTPI	Past President Royal Town Planning Institute
PRA	President of the Royal Academy
PRBS	President, Royal Society of British Sculptors
PRCS	President of the Royal College of Surgeons
PRE	President of the Royal Society of Painter-Etchers and Engravers
PrEng.	Professional Engineer
PRHA	President of the Royal Hibernian Academy
PRI	President of the Royal Institute of Painters in Water Colours
PRIA	President of the Royal Irish Academy
PROI	President of the Royal Institute of Oil Painters
PRS	President of the Royal Society

PRSA	President of the Royal Scottish Academy
PRSE	President of the Royal Society of Edinburgh
PRSH	President of the Royal Society for the Promotion of Health
PRSW	President of the Royal Scottish Water Colour Society
PRUAA	President of the Royal Ulster Academy of Arts
PRWA	President, Royal West of England Academy
PRWS	President of the Royal Society of Painters in Water Colours
PSIAD	President of the Society of Industrial Artists and Designers
PSM	Panglima Setia Mahkota (Malaysia)
PSMA	President of Society of Marine Artists
PVSM	Param Vishishc Seva Medal (India)

Q

QC	Queen's Counsel
QFSM	Queen's Fire Service Medal for Distinguished Service
QGM	Queen's Gallantry Medal
QHC	Queen's Honorary Chaplain
QHDS	Queen's Honorary Dental Surgeon
QHNS	Queen's Honorary Nursing Sister
QHP	Queen's Honorary Physician
QHS	Queen's Honorary Surgeon
QPM	Queen's Police Medal
QRV	Qualified Valuer, Real Estate Institute of New South Wales
QSM	Queen's Service Medal (NZ)
QSO	Queen's Service Order (NZ)

R

RA	Royal Academician
RAM	(Member of) Royal Academy of Music
RBA	Member Royal Society of British Artists
RCA	Member Royal Canadian Academy of Arts
RCamA	Member Royal Cambrian Academy
RD	Royal Navy Reserve Decoration
RDI	Royal Designer for Industry (Royal Society of Arts)
RE	Fellow of Royal Society of Painter-Etchers and Engravers
RGN	Registered General Nurse
RI	Member Royal Institute of Painters in Water Colours
RIBA	Royal Institute of British Architects; *also* Member of the Institute
RMN	Registered Mental Nurse

RNCM	(Member of) Royal Northern College of Music
RNT	Registered Nurse Tutor
ROI	Member Royal Institute of Oil Painters
RP	Member Royal Society of Portrait Painters
RRC	Royal Red Cross
RSA	Royal Scottish Academician
RSCN	Registered Sick Children's Nurse
RSW	Member, Royal Scottish Society of Painters in Water Colours
RWA (RWEA)	Member, Royal West of England Academy
RWS	Member of Royal Society of Painters in Water Colours

S

SB	Bachelor of Science (US)
SBStJ	Serving Brother, Most Venerable Order of the Hospital of St John of Jerusalem
SC	Star of Courage (Canada); Senior Counsel (Eire, Guyana, South Africa)
ScD	Doctor of Science
SCM	State Certified Midwife
SDB	Salesian of Don Bosco
SEN	State Enrolled Nurse
SFInstE	Senior Fellow, Institute of Energy
SFTCD	Senior Fellow, Trinity College Dublin
SGA	Member Society of Graphic Art
SinDrs	Doctor of Chinese
SJ	Society of Jesus (Jesuits)
SJD	Doctor of Juristic Science
SM	Master of Science
SMB	Setia Mahkota Brunei
SMIEEE	Senior Member of Institute of Electrical and Electronics Engineers (New York)
SMIRE	Senior Member Institute of Radio Engineers (New York)
SMN	Seri Maharaja Mangku Negara (Malaysia)
SPCM	Darjah Seri Paduka Cura Si Manja Kini (Malaysia)
SPDK	Seri Panglima Darjal Kinabalu
SPk	Sitara-e-Pakistan
SPMB	Seri Paduka Makhota Brunei
SQA	Sitara-i-Quaid-i-Azam (Pakistan)

SRN	State Registered Nurse
SRP	State Registered Physiotherapist
SSC	Solicitor before Supreme Court (Scotland)
SSF	Society of St Francis
SSJE	Society of St John the Evangelist
SSM	Society of the Sacred Mission; Seri Setia Mahkota (Malaysia)
SSStJ	Serving Sister, Most Venerable Order of the Hospital of St John of Jerusalem
STB	*Sacrae Theologiae Baccalaureus* (Bachelor of Sacred Theology)
STD	*Sacrae Theologiae Doctor* (Doctor of Sacred Theology)
STh	Scholar in Theology
STL	*Sacrae Theologiae Lector* (Reader or a Professor of Sacred Theology)
STM	*Sacrae Theologiae Magister* (Master of Sacred Theology)
STP	*Sacrae Theologiae Professor* (Professor of Divinity, old form of DD)

T

TC	Order of the Trinity Cross (Trinidad and Tobago)
TD	Territorial Efficiency Decoration; Efficiency Decoration (T&AVR) (since April 1967); Teachta Dala (Member of the Dqail, Eire)
TDD	Tubercular Diseases Diploma
TEng(CEI)	Technician Engineer
TeolD	Doctor of Theology
ThL	Theological Licentiate
ThSchol	Scholar in Theology
TSD	Tertiary of St Dominic

U

UJD	*Utriusque Juris Doctor*, Doctor of both Laws (Doctor of Canon and Civil Law)

V

VC	Victoria Cross
VD	Volunteer Officers' Decoration
VG	Vicar-General
VMH	Victoria Medal of Honour (Royal Horticultural Society)
VRD	Royal Naval Volunteer Reserve Officers' Decoration

W

WhSch	Whitworth Scholar
WS	Writer to the Signet

TITLES AND FORMS OF ADDRESS

ROYALTY

Style of Addressing in Speech

On presentation to the Queen the subject does not start the conversation. He or she will answer, using in the first instance the title Your Majesty, and subsequently Ma'am.

For all royal princes the same rules apply, the title used in the first instance being Your Royal Highness, and subsequently Sir. Royal princesses, whether married or unmarried, are called in the first instance Your Royal Highness, and subsequently Ma'am.

Style of Addressing in Writing

The Queen

Madam, *or*
May it please Your Majesty,

I have the honour to remain, Madam,
Your Majesty's most humble and obedient subject,

Address of envelope (for formal or State documents only)—

To The Queen's Most Excellent Majesty,

Otherwise—

To Her Majesty The Queen.

The Duke of Edinburgh

is entitled to the style of a Prince of the Blood Royal, as His Royal Highness The Prince Philip, Duke of Edinburgh.

Queen Mother

Addressing Envelope—

To Her Majesty Queen [Elizabeth the Queen Mother].

Otherwise as for the Queen.

Princes and Princesses of the Blood Royal
Dukes and Duchesses of the Blood Royal

Sir (or Madam),

I have the honour to be, Sir (or Madam),
Your Royal Highness's most humble and obedient servant,

Address of envelope—

To His (or Her) Royal Highness the Prince (or Princess)
————

To His (or Her) Royal Highness the Duke (or Duchess) of
————

A writer not personally known to the Queen or other member of the Royal Family should address his letter to the Private Secretary, Equerry or Lady in Waiting of the person concerned, asking that the subject of the letter be made known to Her Majesty (or to His or Her Royal Highness).

THE PEERAGE

The peerage has five descending grades. They are DUKES, MARQUESSES, EARLS, VISCOUNTS, and BARONS, and in each grade there are five classes. We will take them all in turn, creating a new title in each grade for our examples, but beginning with some general remarks applying to all grades. Rules for each grade separately appear on pages 48, 58, 68, 77 and 84.

Dowagers

These rules apply to the five grades of the peerage and also to the baronetage.

A dowager peeress is the earliest surviving widow of a preceding holder of the title, irrespective of her relationship to the existing holder. She may thus be mother, grandmother, aunt, great-aunt, etc.

Example—The Dowager Duchess of Middlesex.

Socially, however, a dowager peeress may prefer to be known not as Dowager, but by her Christian name; if this is so, she will probably make an announcement in the press of the style she prefers.

Where a Dowager is alive, succeeding widows use their Christian name.

Example.—Mary, Duchess of Middlesex.

If the existing peer has no wife, the widow of his predecessor usually prefers to be addressed as if her husband were still alive, without prefix or Christian name.

When the Dowager dies, the next senior widow becomes the Dowager.

In Scotland the style of Dowager is applied only where the peeress is mother or grandmother of the reigning peer; it is carefully retained in Scottish families, since it emphasizes that the widow became ancestress of an heir.

Former Wives of Peers

The wife of a peer whose marriage has been dissolved uses her Christian name.

> *Example.*—Mary, Duchess of Middlesex.

Peeresses re-marrying

A peeress who re-marries loses the title she acquired by marriage to a peer; but retains or resumes any title she previously bore in her own right, or as the daughter of a peer.

Courtesy Titles

All peers have a family name as well as their titles, although in numerous cases, especially in the lower ranks of the peerage, the two are the same. The family name is used by the sons and daughters of peers, except in the cases of eldest sons of dukes, marquesses, and earls.

In almost every case peers of these three categories have lesser titles also, of which the eldest son usually takes the highest as his courtesy title and uses it in every way as if it were his by right. In the few cases where there are no second titles, as in the earldoms of Devon, Huntingdon, and Temple of Stowe, the family name is used as a courtesy title. The eldest son of a duke is born in the degree of a marquess, but his courtesy title depends upon his father's lesser dignities. He takes the highest of these, which may be only that of an earl, a viscount, or a baron. He takes his title from birth, and, when he marries, his wife becomes a marchioness or a countess, or whatever it may be, and his children take the titles attached to those ranks. The eldest son of an eldest son takes a third title from the ducal collection, but of a lower grade than that of his father.

The correct ways of using these titles will be found under their various headings. They are in all respects the same, whether they are actual or courtesy titles, except that the prefixes, Most Honourable and Right Honourable, or The (which stands in their place; *see* p. 45), are not used for courtesy titles.

Peerage of Scotland

The Peerage of Scotland (that is, peerages created in Scotland before the Act of Union of 1707) has two distinctive features. The lowest grade of the peerage is not Baron (which in Scots law denotes the property of a territorial estate held by Baronial charter), but Lord of Parliament. This should not be confused with the judicial title given to a Judge of the Court of Session in Scotland(*see* p. 172). In practice the difference has little effect, since Barons are known and addressed as Lord in any case; but where it is desired to show the exact title, it is, in the case of Scottish lordships created before 1707, not Baron Gray (for example), but Lord Gray. Scottish Lords and Ladies and their families are addressed in all ways the same as Barons and Baronesses (*see* p. 84), with the exception which follows.

The second feature peculiar to Scottish peerages is the title of Master given to the heir, whether apparent or presumptive (also to the eldest son of an heir who bears a courtesy title). The heir to a Duke, a Marquess or an Earl who is entitled to use a courtesy title will do so, rather than be known as Master of ————; but the heir to a Viscount or Lord, and the eldest son of a Viscount or Lord by courtesy, is known as Master. The title is nearly always derived from that to which the bearer is heir; thus Viscount Falkland's heir is the Master of Falkland, and Lord Napier and Ettrick's the Master of Napier. Their wives are called The Hon. Mrs ————, without the husband's Christian name.

> *Example.*—The Master of Ballantrae.
> The Hon. Mrs Scott of Ballantrae.

Style of Addressing in Speech

Formerly styled "My Lord", the Master is nowadays called Sir on formal occasions, otherwise by his surname, Mr Scott. In the household and family he is referred to as The Master, and servants address him as Master. His wife is called Mrs Scott.

Style of Addressing in Writing

The formal manner is:

> Sir (or Dear Sir),

> *Address of envelope*—

>> The Master of Ballantrae.

> Madam,

> *Address of envelope*—

>> The Hon. Mrs Scott of Ballantrae.

The social manner of address in writing is:

> Dear Mr Scott,

> *Address of envelope*—

>> The Master of Ballantrae.

> Dear Mrs Scott,

> *Address of envelope*—

>> The Hon. Mrs Scott of Ballantrae.

Collaterals

All courtesy titles, or titles connected with the family name of a peer, are attached only to the actual descendants of that peer, with one occasional exception. It is that when a peer is succeeded by other than a son, the new peer's brothers and sisters may take the titles that would have been theirs if their father had succeeded.* In such cases he *would* have succeeded had he lived, so the honour really comes through him. His widow, however, if he has left one, does not share this privilege.

For instance, the 8th Duke of Devonshire died without issue. His heir was the eldest son of his brother, Lord Edward Cavendish, who had predeceased him. As long as the 8th duke lived his heir presumptive had no title, nor of course had his two brothers. But when Mr Victor Cavendish succeeded to the dukedom, his brothers became Lord Richard and Lord John Cavendish. His mother, however, remained Lady Edward Cavendish.

* These privileges cannot be claimed as a right. They are given by favour of the Crown, and warrants are granted in such cases only upon the recommendation of the Home Secretary.

Addressing the Heir on Succession

It is customary to continue to address the heir of a peerage or a baronetcy, when the peer or baronet dies, by the courtesy title or other style by which he was formerly known until after his predecessor's funeral.

New Peerages

When a new peerage is created, it is not possible to address the new peer as Lord ———— immediately, because his title must be decided and the Letters Patent prepared. The new title will then be gazetted. If Mr John Smith receives a peerage, he remains Mr Smith until he becomes, e.g., Baron Smith of Newtown; he cannot be called by any title until his actual title is known. (But *see* p. 103 for new knighthoods, etc.).

Life Peers

Life peers rank with hereditary barons and baronesses according to the date of their creation. Wives of life peers take the title of

Lady, and their children The Honourable. Husbands of women life peers do not take any title. Children of women life peers, however, take the title The Honourable. In all respects, except that the title does not descend, rules as for BARONS and BARONESSES apply (*see* p. 84).

Disclaiming of Hereditary Peerages

The Peerage Act of 1963 authorized the disclaimer for life of certain hereditary peerages. A peer who disclaims his peerage loses all titles and precedence attached to it; he cannot however disclaim a baronetcy or a knighthood, and if he possesses one will be known by the appropriate title. His wife also loses the title and precedence which she received from her husband's hereditary peerage, although not, of course, any title and precedence she may herself have possessed. The eldest son of a disclaimed peer may continue if he wishes to use the courtesy title he used previously, and other children to use the titles Lord, Lady or The Honourable.

Peeresses in Their Own Right

Some baronies and a few earldoms descend in the female line. A peeress in her own right is addressed exactly as though the rank were obtained through marriage.

Husbands and Children of Peeresses in Their Own Right

Husbands take no style or dignity from their wives. Their children, however, are in all respects as if the peerage were held by their father.

Husbands and Children of Peers' Daughters

A husband's name or status is not altered in any way by his wife's degree, and the children have no distinctions of any sort through their mother.

Devolving Titles

A hereditary title descends only in the oldest direct line, that is from father to son, or grandfather to grandson, except in such instances as those already mentioned, in which descent also includes the female line, and those in which remainder is expressly granted. In the case of an ancient peerage, succession sometimes devolves upon a distant cousin, but he succeeds not because he is a cousin of the preceding peer, but because he is descended from some former holder of the title. The brother or nephew of a newly created peer would not succeed to his honours unless special remainder were granted to his Patent, nor would a cousin of an older creation, unless his descent were from a former holder of it. This explains why some peers succeeding take lower titles than their predecessors. The 9th Earl of Drogheda, for instance, gained the title through descent from the fifth earl. The sixth earl was raised to the marquessate, which was held also by the seventh and eighth earls, as his direct descendants. But with the death of the third marquess the direct male descent from the first died out, though descent from previous holders of the lower title did not.

The Prefix "The"

Members of the Peerage are entitled by ancient custom, almost amounting to a right, to the following appellations:

> Dukes—The Most Noble.
> Marquesses—The Most Honourable.
> Other Peers—The Right Honourable.

The practice is not to make use of the full title of Peers when referring to them, but to shorten the prefix to "The" as "The Duke of Norfolk".

The use of "The Lord" is really short for "The Right Hon. Lord". When "Lord" is used without a prefix it is for a courtesy title.

Where any Peer is entitled to the additional prefix of Right Honourable by virtue of a Privy Counsellorship (*see* p. 116), the addition merges in that attaching to the existing title; but Dukes and Marquesses retain the right to both their designations in legal documents and formal circumstances. "The Right Hon." should not be shortened to "The" (as above) when a Peer is also a Privy Counsellor; his membership of the Privy Council entitles him to the full prefix at all times. Membership of the Privy Council being an office and not an honour, the initials P.C. should not be appended to any name or title (and *see* pp. 180–181).

The Title "Lady"

This is probably the commonest of all, as it is used of all peeresses under the rank of duchess, of all daughters of the three highest ranks of the peerage, and of the wives of baronets and knights. The prefix "The" was once by general custom used in addressing the daughters of dukes, marquesses and earls, e.g. "The Lady Jean Smith". The practice existed only by courtesy, and was not recognized as correct by, for example, the College of Arms; it is no longer generally used, although it would be wrong to deprive elderly ladies of the prefix should they feel strongly about it. Ladies do not retain their husbands' titles on re-marriage to commoners.

The Title "Honourable"

This title is a fairly frequent one, including as it does the younger sons of earls, all the sons and daughters of viscounts and barons, and the wives of the sons, besides its use outside the ranks of the peerage. The important rule to note is that it is *never* used in speech. Neither is it used in letter-writing, except on the envelope. (*See also* p. 165, for uses outside the peerage.)

Territorial Additions

All peerages have still, as in their origin, a territorial basis, which is expressed in the Letters Patent creating a new peerage, as BARON SMITH, of (a place with which the new Baron has connections) in the County of —————. This, which may be described as the "address" of the peerage, does not form part of the title, and should never be used as though it did. Some peerages, however, have a territorial addition included in their titles, to avoid confusion with older peerages of the same name (whether or not these still survive). In these cases, of which the Baronies of Morris, Morris of Borth-y-Gest, Morris of Grasmere, and Morris of Kenwood make a good example, the Letters Patent will read e.g. BARON MORRIS OF GRASMERE, of Grasmere in the County of Westmorland, and it will be clear that the territorial addition forms part of the title, and should be used in addressing or referring to the peer. It is not possible for peers to change their titles from the form in which they were first created.

(*See also* p. 106 for the Scottish use of territorial additions.)

DUKES AND DUCHESSES

To help us in our explanation we will create a Duke of Middlesex, who is also Marquess of Huddersfield and Earl of Ramsgate, to name only his prinicpal titles. His family name shall be Smith.

The titles of all existing dukedoms are taken from the name of a place. (There are no instances of the title being taken from the family name. In those cases where the two are the same, the family name has been taken from the place.)

> *Example.*—The Duke of Middlesex.
> The Duchess of Middlesex.

Style of Addressing in Speech

The formal style of a Duke is "The Most Noble the Duke of . . .", but the form of address for those of social equality is Duke of Middlesex or Duchess of Middlesex, though the necessity for using the full title would generally be avoided. For instance, if there is no need to distinguish between different dukes and duchesses, plain Duke or Duchess is correct. They are referred to as The Duke or The Duchess. But in conversation it is best to make as sparing a use as possible of titles. Formally addressed as Your Grace, they are referred to as His Grace and Her Grace.

The archaic style of the title in conjunction with a Christian name, as Duke John, is not now used. To distinguish a particular duke from others of his line he is called John, Duke of ————, or The second Duke of ————.

A dowager duchess is so called when she is the earliest surviving widow of a preceding duke irrespective of her relationship to the reigning duke (but *see* p. 39 for Scottish practice). Later surviving widows are distinguished by the use of their Christian name before the title (*see* p. 39).

Examples.—The Dowager Duchess of Middlesex.
Mary, Duchess of Middlesex.

Bùt if the existing duke has no wife, the widow of his predecessor is addressed in all respects as if her husband were alive.

Example.—The Duchess of Middlesex.

The rules for addressing in speech are in all ways the same as for the duke's wife, but if confusion were threatened she would be referred to as The Dowager Duchess.

Style of Addressing in Writing

The most formal manner of address in writing is:

My Lord Duke,
> I remain,
>> Your Grace's most obedient servant,

Address of envelope—
> His Grace the Duke of Middlesex.

Madam,
> I remain,
>> Your Grace's most obedient servant,

Address of envelope—
> Her Grace the Duchess of Middlesex.

Less formally, but still not socially:

My Lord Duke,
> Yours faithfully,

Address of envelope—
> His Grace the Duke of Middlesex.

Madam,
> Yours faithfully,

Address of envelope—

> Her Grace the Duchess of Middlesex.

(To a Dowager.)

Madam,

> I remain,
>> Your Grace's most obedient servant,

or

Madam,

> Yours faithfully.

Address of envelope—

> Her Grace the Dowager Duchess of Middlesex, *or*
> Her Grace Mary, Duchess of Middlesex.

(To a Former Wife.)

Madam,

> I remain, Madam,
>> Your most obedient servant,

or

Madam,

> Yours faithfully,

Address of envelope—

> Mary, Duchess of Middlesex.

The social manner of address in writing is:

> Dear Duke of Middlesex,
>> Yours sincerely,

or more familiarly

Dear Duke,

> Yours sincerely,

Address of envelope—

    His Grace the Duke of Middlesex.

Dear Duchess of Middlesex,
                Yours sincerely,

           or more familiarly

Dear Duchess,

           Yours sincerely,

Address of envelope—

    Her Grace the Duchess of Middlesex.

        (To a Dowager.)

Dear Duchess of Middlesex,
                Yours sincerely,

           or more familiarly

Dear Duchess,

           Yours sincerely,

Address of envelope—

    Her Grace the Dowager Duchess of Middlesex, *or*
    Her Grace Mary, Duchess of Middlesex.

In social address the prefix His Grace or Her Grace may be omitted from the envelope.

        (To a Former Wife.)

Dear Duchess of Middlesex,
                Yours sincerely,

           or more familiarly

Dear Duchess,

           Yours sincerely,

Address of envelope—
> Mary, Duchess of Middlesex.

Eldest Sons of Dukes

(*See also under* COURTESY TITLES, p. 40)

The eldest son of a duke is born in the degree of a marquess, but his courtesy title depends upon his father's lesser dignities. He normally takes the highest of these, which may be only that of an earl or lesser degree. He takes his title from birth, and, when he marries, his wife and children share the honours attached to his rank. His eldest son takes a third title from the ducal collection, of a lower grade than that of his father.

Example.—The eldest son of our Duke of Middlesex would be Marquess of Huddersfield and his wife Marchioness of Huddersfield. Their eldest son would be Earl of Ramsgate.

The correct use of these titles will be found under their various headings. It is in all respects the same, whether they are actual or courtesy titles, except that the prefix Most Honourable, or "The", which represents it, is not used, i.e. Marquess of Huddersfield, not The Most Honourable the Marquess of Huddersfield. (*See* p. 45.)

Daughters and Younger Sons of Dukes

The younger sons of a duke bear the title "Lord" with their Christian and family names, and all daughters of a duke bear the title "Lady".

> *Example.*—Lord John Smith.
> Lady Barbara Smith.

Style of Addressing in Speech

In this category the commonest mistakes are made by those who do not know the distinctions between the sorts of people who are entitled to be called "Lord" or "Lady". Lord John Smith must *never* be called Lord Smith, nor Lady Barbara Smith Lady Smith. When the full titles are not used they are called Lord John and Lady Barbara. There is no other abbreviation unless one is on such terms of intimacy as to use their Christian names alone.

Style of Addressing in Writing

The most formal manner of address in writing is:

> My Lord,
> > I have the honour to remain,
> > > Your Lordship's Obedient servant,

Address of envelope—
> Lord John Smith.

> My Lady (or Madam),
> > I have the honour to remain,
> > > Your Ladyship's obedient servant,

Address of envelope—
> Lady Barbara Smith.

Less formally, but still not socially:

> My Lord,
> > Yours faithfully,

Address of envelope—
> Lord John Smith.

> Madam,
> > Yours faithfully,

Address of envelope—
> Lady Barbara Smith.

The social manner of address in writing is:

Dear Lord John Smith,
                              Yours sincerely,

                        or more familiarly

Dear Lord John,
                              Yours sincerely,

Address of envelope—
          Lord John Smith.

Dear Lady Barbara Smith,
                              Yours sincerely,

                        or more familiarly

Dear Lady Barbara,
                              Yours sincerely,

Address of envelope—
          Lady Barbara Smith.

Wives of Younger Sons of Dukes

The mistake already alluded to in this category is made most often of all in the case of wives of younger sons of dukes and marquesses. The wife of Lord John Smith is Lady John Smith, and never in any circumstances Lady Smith. She is known less formally as Lady John. This rule is varied only when she is of higher rank than her husband, in which case her own Christian name is substituted for his. (*See under* MARRIED DAUGHTERS OF DUKES, p. 56.)

Style of Addressing in Writing

The most formal manner is:

Madam (or My Lady),
> I have the honour to remain,
>> Your Ladyship's obedient servant,

Address of envelope—
> Lady John Smith.

Less formally, but still not socially:

Madam,
> Yours faithfully,

Address of envelope—
> Lady John Smith.

The social manner of address in writing is:

Dear Lady John Smith,
> Yours sincerely,

> *or more familiarly*

Dear Lady John,
> Yours sincerely,

Address of envelope—
> Lady John Smith.

Widows of Younger Sons of Dukes

If the widow of a younger son of a duke, having no title of her own, re-marries, she may not continue to use her late husband's name and title. If, on the other hand, she has a title of her own, she will use it coupled with her new name. If she re-marries into the peerage, she will obviously share her second husband's name and title. The same rules apply to former wives as to widows.

Children of Younger Sons of Dukes

The children of younger sons of dukes have no distinctions of any
sort. All the sons and daughters of Lord and Lady John Smith
would be plain Mr or Miss. A popular fallacy would make them
honourables, but that is quite wrong. They have, of course, some
precedence in the social scale.

Married Daughters of Dukes

The daughter of a duke, in marrying a peer (not a courtesy peer),
shares her husband's title and precedence. In all other cases she
retains her own title of Lady with her Christian name even if she
marries the younger son of a duke, because by a curious anomaly
all peers' daughters rank one degree higher than younger sons of
the same grade. In the event of marriage with the heir of an earl
or lesser peer, she is entitled, if she prefers it, to retain her own
title while her husband is a courtesy lord, because she actually
keeps her precedence until he succeeds to his peerage. There are
instances of both usages in the peerage, and the chosen style
should be ascertained in each case. Marriage with a commoner
does not alter her rank in any way (nor, incidentally, that of her
husband). Our duke's daughter, Lady Barbara Smith, married to
Mr Peter Green, would become Lady Barbara Green. In no
circumstances would she be called Lady Peter Green. Together
they would be referred to as Mr Peter and Lady Barbara Green,
or Mr and Lady Barbara Green. Curiously enough, however, the
daughter of a duke (as also of a marquess or earl) keeps her rank
as such in the table of precedence if she marries out of the
peerage, but exchanges it for that of her husband if she remains in
it, even if it means descending several steps. Thus Lady Barbara,
having married Mr Peter Green, would go in to dinner before a
sister who had married a baron.

Examples.—Marriage with

A commoner	Peter Green, Esq.	Lady Barbara Green
Scottish chief or laird	James MacBrown of Glenbrown	Lady Barbara MacBrown of Glenbrown
A knight or baronet	Sir Bernard Brown	Lady Barbara Brown
A younger son of an earl or lesser peer	The Honourable George Wilson	Lady Barbara Wilson
An eldest son of an earl	Viscount Staines (Lord Staines)	Lady Barbara Staines, *or* Viscountess Staines (Lady Staines), as she prefers
A younger son of a duke or marquess	Lord John Bull	Lady Barbara Bull
An eldest son of a marquess	Earl of Malvern (Lord Malvern)	Countess of Malvern (Lady Malvern) *or* Lady Barbara Malvern, as she prefers
An eldest son of a duke	Marquess of Mere (Lord Mere)	Marchioness of Mere (Lady Mere)
A peer of any rank	The Right Hon. Lord Slough (The Lord Slough)	The Right Hon. Lady Slough (The Lady Slough)

Children of Daughters of Dukes

The children of daughters of dukes receive no titles or distinctions of any sort through their mother.

MARQUESSES AND MARCHIONESSES

This title is rendered in two ways, marquess or marquis. The former is the older and purely British. Peers of this rank use which form they prefer, and their choice should be ascertained and observed in addressing them.

Our typical peer of this, the second grade, shall be the Marquess of Montgomeryshire, who is also the Earl of Malvern and Baron Swindon. His family name shall be Evans.

Territorial Titles

The title of marquess is generally taken from the name of a place, as it invariably is in the case of a duke.

Example.—The Marquess of Montgomeryshire.

There are two marquessates in our peerage, however, whose titles are taken from the family names, and in both these cases the preposition is dropped, thus:

> The Marquess Conyngham.
> The Marquess Townshend.

These two are the only instances in the marquessate of titles taken from family names, but in two other cases the preposition is dropped even though the titles are territorial, viz.,

> The Marquess Camden.
> The Marquess Douro.

Style of Addressing in Speech

It has been said already that all peers and peeresses below ducal rank are called lord and lady in speech. This brings us to a mistake quite commonly made in connection with the lower grades of the peerage. Although it is correct to talk of the Duke, or Duchess of Middlesex—indeed, they could not be referred to in any other way—the rule is quite different for the marquessate. The Marquess and Marchioness of Montgomeryshire would always be referred and spoken to as Lord and Lady Montgomeryshire. There are a few formal occasions on which the full title would be used, but it would never occur in intimate speech.

Style of Addressing in Writing

The most formal manner is:

> My Lord Marquess,   *or*
> My Lord,
> > I have the honour to be,
> > > Your Lordship's obedient servant,

Address of envelope—

> The Most Hon. the Marquess of Montgomeryshire.

Madam,
> I have the honour to remain,
> > Your Ladyship's obedient servant,

Address of envelope—

> The Most Hon. the Marchioness of Montgomeryshire.

Less formally, but still not socially:

> My Lord,
> > Yours faithfully,

Address of envelope—

> The Most Hon. the Marquess of Montgomeryshire.

Madam,
> Yours faithfully,

Address of envelope—
> The Most Hon. the Marchioness of Montgomeryshire.

The social manner of address in writing is:
> Dear Lord Montgomeryshire, *or*
> Dear Montgomeryshire,
>> Yours sincerely,

Address of envelope—
> The Marquess of Montgomeryshire.

> Dear Lady Montgomeryshire,
>> Yours sincerely,

Address of envelope—
> The Marchioness of Montgomeryshire.

Dowager Marchionesses

A dowager marchioness is so called when she is the earliest surviving widow of a preceding marquess, irrespective of her relationship to the reigning marquess (but *see* p. 39 for Scottish practice). A later surviving widow is distinguished by the use of her Christian name before her title (*see* p. 39).

> *Examples.*—The Dowager Marchioness of Montgomery-
>> shire.
> Enid, Marchioness of Montgomeryshire.

Style of Addressing in Writing

The most formal manner is:
> Madam,
>> I have the honour to remain,
>>> Your Ladyship's obedient servant,

Less formally:

>Madam,

>>Yours faithfully,

>*Address of envelope*—

>>The Most Hon. the Dowager Marchioness of Mont-
gomeryshire, *or*
>>The Most Hon. Enid, Marchioness of Montgomeryshire.

The social manner of address in writing is:

>Dear Lady Montgomeryshire,

>>Yours sincerely,

>*Address of envelope*—

>>The Dowager Marchioness of Montgomeryshire, *or*
>>Enid, Marchioness of Montgomeryshire.

The former wife of a Marquess uses her Christian name before
the title.

Style of Addressing in Writing

The most formal manner is:

>Madam,

>>I have the honour to remain,

>>>Your Ladyship's obedient servant,

Less formally:

>Madam,

>>Yours faithfully,

>*Address of envelope* (in each case)—

>>Enid, Marchioness of Montgomeryshire.

The social manner of address in writing is:

>Dear Lady Montgomeryshire,

>>Yours sincerely,

Address of envelope—
Enid, Marchioness of Montgomeryshire.

Eldest Sons of Marquesses
(*See also under* COURTESY TITLES, p. 40)

As stated elsewhere, peers in this category have lesser titles as well, and the eldest son takes usually the highest of these as his courtesy title, which is used in every way as if it were his by right. He takes the title from birth, and on his marriage his wife and children share the honours attached to his rank. His eldest son would take a third title from among the marquess's lesser titles.

Example.—The eldest son of our Marquess of Montgomeryshire would be Earl of Malvern and his wife Countess of Malvern. Their eldest son would be Baron Swindon. The correct use of these titles will be found under their various headings. It is in all respects the same, whether they are actual or courtesy titles, except that the prefix Right Honourable, or "The", which represents it, is not used, i.e.

Earl of Malvern (*see* p. 45).

Daughters and Younger Sons of Marquesses

The younger sons of a marquess bear the title Lord with their Christian and family names, and all daughters of a marquess bear the title Lady.

Example.—Lord Charles Evans.
Lady Joan Evans.

Style of Addressing in Speech

In this category the commonest mistakes are made. Lord Charles Evans must never be called Lord Evans nor Lady Joan Evans Lady Evans. When the full titles are not used, they are called Lord Charles and Lady Joan. There is no other abbreviation.

Style of Addressing in Writing

The most formal manner of address in writing is:

My Lord,
> I have the honour to remain,
>> Your Lordship's obedient servant,

Address of envelope—
> Lord Charles Evans.

Madam (or My Lady),
> I have the honour to remain,
>> Your Ladyship's obedient servant,

Address of envelope—
> Lady Joan Evans.

Less formally, but still not socially:

My Lord,
> Yours faithfully,

Address of envelope—
> Lord Charles Evans.

Madam,
> Yours faithfully,

Address of envelope—
> Lady Joan Evans.

The social manner of address in writing is:

Dear Lord Charles Evans,
> Yours sincerely,

or more familiarly

Dear Lord Charles,
> Yours sincerely,

Address of envelope—
>   Lord Charles Evans.

Dear Lady Joan Evans,
>   Yours sincerely,

>   *or more familiarly*

Dear Lady Joan,
>   Yours sincerely,

Address of envelope—
>   Lady Joan Evans.

Wives of Younger Sons of Marquesses

The mistake already alluded to in this category is made most often of all in the case of wives of younger sons of dukes and marquesses. The wife of Lord Charles Evans is Lady Charles Evans, and never in any circumstances Lady Evans. She is known less formally as Lady Charles. This rule is varied only when she is of higher rank than her husband, in which case her own Christian name is substituted for his. (*See under* MARRIED DAUGHTERS OF MARQUESSES, p. 65.)

Style of Addressing in Writing

The most formal manner is:
>   Madam (or My Lady),
>   I have the honour to remain,
>   Your Ladyship's obedient servant,

Address of envelope—
>   Lady Charles Evans.

Less formally:
>   Madam,

>   Yours faithfully,

Address of envelope—
> Lady Charles Evans.

The social manner of address in writing is:
> Dear Lady Charles Evans,
>> Yours sincerely,

or more familiarly

> Dear Lady Charles,
>> Yours sincerely,

Address of envelope—
> Lady Charles Evans.

Widows of Younger Sons of Marquesses

If the widow of a younger son of a marquess, having no title of her own, re-marries she may not continue to use her late husband's name and title. If, on the other hand, she has a title of her own, she will use it coupled with her new name. The same rules apply to former wives as to widows.

Children of Younger Sons of Marquesses

The children of younger sons of marquesses have no distinctions of any sort. All the sons and daughters of Lord and Lady Charles Evans would be plain Mr and Miss. They have, of course, some precedence in the social scale.

Married Daughters of Marquesses

The daughter of a marquess, in marrying a peer (not a courtesy peer), shares her husband's title and precedence, as also if she marries a man of equal or higher rank than her own—the eldest son of a marquess or any son of a duke. In all other cases she retains her own title of Lady with her Christian name, even if she

marries the younger son of a marquess, because, as stated
elsewhere, all peers' daughters rank one degree higher than
younger sons of the same grade. In the event of marriage with the
heir of an earl or lesser peer, she is entitled, if she prefers it, to
retain her own title while her husband is a courtesy lord, because
she actually keeps her precedence until he succeeds to his
peerage. There are instances of both usages in the peerage, and
the chosen style should be ascertained in each case. Marriage
with a commoner does not alter her rank in any way (nor,
incidentally, that of her husband). Our marquess's daughter,
married to Mr Peter Green, would become Lady Joan Green. In
no circumstances would she be called Lady Peter Green.
Together they would be described as Mr Peter and Lady Joan
Green. Curiously enough, however, the daughter of a marquess
(as also of a duke or earl) keeps her rank as such in the table of
precedence if she marries out of the peerage, but exchanges it for
that of her husband if she remains in it, even if it means
descending several steps. Thus Lady Joan, having married Mr
Peter Green, would go in to dinner before a sister who had
married a baron.

Examples.—Marriage with

A commoner	Peter Green, Esq.	Lady Joan Green
A knight or baronet	Sir Bernard Brown	Lady Joan Brown
A younger son of an earl or lesser peer	The Honourable George Wilson	Lady Joan Wilson
An eldest son of an earl	Viscount Staines (Lord Staines)	Lady Joan Staines, *or* Viscountess Staines (Lady Staines), as she prefers
A younger son of a marquess	Lord John Bull	Lady Joan Bull
A younger son of a duke	Lord John Smith	Lady John Smith, *or* Lady Joan Smith, as she prefers
An eldest son of a marquess	Earl of Malvern (Lord Malvern)	Countess of Malvern (Lady Malvern)

| An eldest son of a duke | Marquess of Mere (Lord Mere) | Marchioness of Mere (Lady Mere) |
| A peer of any rank | The Right Hon. Lord Slough (The Lord Slough) | The Right Hon. Lady Slough (The Lady Slough) |

Children of Daughters of Marquesses

The children of daughters of marquesses receive no titles or distinctions of any sort through their mother.

EARLS AND COUNTESSES

This grade is sometimes territorial, sometimes taken from the family name. In the former case the preposition "of" is generally used, and in the latter case it is not, although there are numerous exceptions to both rules.

In one or two instances, such as the Earl of Winchilsea and Nottingham, two separate earldoms have become merged. Both titles are used on all formal occasions and even on the social envelope. But in social speech and letters only the first one is employed. The Earl of Winchilsea and Nottingham's title provides an instance of the little traps which are sometimes, almost perversely it would seem, set for the unwary. The name of the ancient town from which Lord Winchilsea takes his title is spelt Winchelsea. Another curious instance is that the town of Beaconsfield, from which Disraeli took his title, is pronounced Beckonsfield. He lived within a few miles of it at Hughenden, and must have been aware of this. But his title was pronounced by him as it is written, and continues to be so pronounced.

Our typical peer in this, the third grade, shall be the Earl of Whitby, with a second title, Viscount Staines, and the family name of Collins.

Style of Addressing in Speech

It has been remarked already that all peers and peeresses below ducal rank are called lord and lady in speech. This rule applies, of course, to earls and countesses, who are always referred and spoken to as lord and lady. As in the case of the marquessate, there are a few formal occasions on which the full title would be used, but it would never happen in intimate speech.

Style of Addressing in Writing

The most formal manner is:

My Lord,
I have the honour to remain,
Your Lordship's obedient servant,

Address of envelope—
The Right Hon. the Earl of Whitby.

Madam,
I have the honour to remain,
Your Ladyship's obedient servant,

Address of envelope—
The Right Hon. the Countess of Whitby.

Less formally, but still not socially:

My Lord,
Yours faithfully,

Address of envelope—
The Right Hon. the Earl of Whitby.

Madam,
Yours faithfully,

Address of envelope—
The Right Hon. the Countess of Whitby.

The social manner of address in writing is:

Dear Lord Whitby, *or*
Dear Whitby,
Yours sincerely,

Address of envelope—
The Earl of Whitby.

Dear Lady Whitby,
>Yours sincerely,

Address of envelope—
>The Countess of Whitby.

Dowager Countesses

A dowager countess is so called when she is the earliest surviving widow of a preceding earl (but *see* p. 39 for Scottish practice). A later surviving widow is distinguished by the use of the Christian name before her title (*see* p. 39).

>The Dowager Countess of Whitby.
>Muriel, Countess of Whitby.

Style of Addressing in Speech

is exactly the same as if she were the reigning countess.

Style of Addressing in Writing

The most formal manner is:

>Madam,
>>I have the honour to remain,
>>>Your Ladyship's obedient servant,

Less formally:

>Madam,
>>Yours faithfully,

Address of envelope—

>The Right Hon. the Dowager Countess of Whitby,   *or*
>The Right Hon. Muriel, Countess of Whitby.

The social manner of address in writing is:

>Dear Lady Whitby,
>>Yours sincerely,

Address of envelope—

> The Dowager Countess of Whitby,   *or*
> Muriel, Countess of Whitby.

The former wife of an Earl uses her Christian name before the title.

Style of Addressing in Writing

The most formal manner is:

> Madam,
>
> I have the honour to remain,
>   Your Ladyship's obedient servant,

Less formally:

> Madam,
>
>   Yours faithfully,

Address of envelope—

> Muriel, Countess of Whitby.

The social manner of address in writing is:

> Dear Lady Whitby,
>   Yours sincerely,

Address of envelope—

> Muriel, Countess of Whitby.

Eldest Sons of Earls

(See also under Courtesy Titles, p. 40)

As stated elsewhere, peers in this category have lesser titles as well, and the eldest son takes usually the highest of these as his courtesy title, which is used in every way as if it were his by right. He takes the title from birth, and on his marriage his wife and children share the honours attached to his rank.

Example.—The eldest son of our Earl of Whitby would be Viscount Staines and his wife Viscountess Staines. The correct use of these titles will be found under their various headings. It is in all respects the same whether they are actual or courtesy titles, with the exception that the prefix Right Honourable, or "The", which represents it, is not used, i.e. Viscount Staines. (*See* p. 45.)

Daughters of Earls

Daughters of earls bear the title Lady with their Christian and family names.

Example.—Lady Violet Collins.

Style of Addressing in Speech

The same rules apply as in the case of daughters of dukes and marquesses, viz. when the full title is not used, our earl's daughter will be called Lady Violet. There is no other abbreviation unless one is on such terms of intimacy as to use the Christian name alone.

Style of Addressing in Writing

The most formal manner is:

> Madam (or My Lady),
> > I have the honour to remain,
> > > Your Ladyship's obedient servant,

Less formally:
> Madam,
> > Yours faithfully,

Address of envelope—
> Lady Violet Collins.

The social manner of address in writing is:

> Dear Lady Violet Collins,
>> Yours sincerely,

or more familiarly

> Dear Lady Violet,
>> Yours sincerely,

Address of envelope—
> Lady Violet Collins.

Younger Sons of Earls

Unlike the higher grades of the peerage, younger sons of earls are styled Honourable with their Christian and family names (not initials), and there is nothing to distinguish them from the sons of viscounts and barons.

> *Example.*—The Honourable Thomas Collins.

Style of Addressing in Speech

As remarked elsewhere, this title is never used in speech or letter-writing, except on the envelope. The younger sons of earls are called Mr, always in conjunction with the Christian name.

> *Example.*—Mr Thomas Collins.

The title is never printed on visiting-cards, so that without inner knowledge it is difficult to recognize the rank. When it is desired to indicate it, however, a reference to the holder's parentage would be permissible. Servants would announce the younger son of an earl as Mr Thomas Collins.

Style of Addressing in Writing

The most formal manner is:

Sir,
>> I have the honour to be,
>> >> Your obedient servant,

Less formally:
> Dear Sir,
>> Yours faithfully,

> *Address of envelope—*
>> The Hon. Thomas Collins.

The social manner of address in writing is:
> Dear Mr Collins,
>> Yours sincerely,

> *Address of envelope—*
>> The Hon. Thomas Collins.

Wives of Younger Sons of Earls
share their husbands' title.

> *Example.*—The Hon. Mrs Thomas Collins.

It should be carefully noted that whereas it is wrong to use the designations Mr or Miss with this title, it is right to use the designation Mrs with it. The title is never used in speech, even by a servant, and the wife of Mr Thomas Collins is always alluded to as Mrs Thomas Collins. If she happens to be of higher rank than her husband, she would use her own title in conjunction with her husband's name—without the Honourable.

Style of Addressing in Writing

The most formal manner is:
> Madam,
>> I have the honour to remain,
>> >> Your obedient servant,

Less formally:

> Dear Madam,
>
> > Yours faithfully,

Address of envelope—
> The Hon. Mrs Thomas Collins.

The social manner of address in writing is:

> Dear Mrs Collins,
>
> > Yours sincerely,

Address of envelope—
> The Hon. Mrs Thomas Collins.

Widows of Younger Sons of Earls

keep their title until re-marriage, when it is abandoned in favour of the second husband's status, whether it be higher or lower. If the widow possesses a title in her own right she will of course continue to use it. The same rules apply to former wives as to widows.

Children of Younger Sons of Earls

have no distinction of any sort. They have, of course, a certain social precedence.

Married Daughters of Earls

The daughter of an earl, if she marries a peer (not a courtesy peer), or a man of equal or higher rank than her own, shares her husband's title and precedence. Otherwise she retains her own title of Lady with her Christian name, even if she marries the younger son of an earl, because, as stated elsewhere, all peers' daughters rank one degree higher than younger sons of the same grade. In the event of marriage with the heir of a viscount or lesser peer, she is entitled, if she prefers it, to retain her own title until her husband succeeds to his peerage, because she actually keeps her own precedence until then. In such a case the chosen style should be ascertained. Marriage with a commoner does not alter her rank in any way—nor, incidentally, that of her husband. Our earl's daughter, married to Mr Peter Green, would become Lady Violet Green. She must never be called Lady Peter Green. Together they would be described as Mr Peter and Lady Violet Green. Curiously enough, however, the daughter of an earl keeps her rank as such in the table of predecence if she marries out of the peerage, but exchanges it for that of her husband if she remains in it, even if it means descending several steps. Thus Lady Violet, having married Mr Peter Green, would go in to dinner before a sister who had married a baron.

Examples.—Marriage with

A commoner	Mr Peter Green	Lady Violet Green
A knight or baronet	Sir Bernard Brown	Lady Violet Brown
A younger son of an earl or lesser peer	The Honourable Michael O'Mara	Lady Violet O'Mara
An eldest son of an earl	Viscount Staines (Lord Staines)	Viscountess Staines (Lady Staines)
A younger son of a marquess	Lord John Bull	Lady John Bull
A younger son of a duke	Lord John Smith	Lady John Smith
An eldest son of a marquess	Earl of Malvern (Lord Malvern)	Countess of Malvern (Lady Malvern)
An eldest son of a duke	Marquess of Mere (Lord Mere)	Marchioness of Mere (Lady Mere)
A peer of any rank	The Right Hon. Lord Slough (The Lord Slough)	The Right Hon. Lady Slough (The Lady Slough)

Children of Daughters of Earls

The children of daughters of earls receive no titles or distinctions of any sort through their mother.

VISCOUNTS AND VISCOUNTESSES

This title is sometimes territorial, sometimes derived from the family name, but in neither case is the preposition "of" used between the style and the title, e.g. Viscount Hereford, not The Viscount of Hereford. Viscounts in the peerage of Scotland (or before 1707) *do* include the "of", e.g. The Viscount of Arbuthnott. A number of Viscounts recently created also contain a territorial addition to the title, e.g. Viscount Grey of Fallodon. In such cases the full style is used on formal occasions and in addressing all letters, formal and social.

Our example in this, the fourth grade of the peerage, shall be Viscount O'Mara, with the same family name.

Style of Addressing in Speech

The rule already explained, that all peers and peeresses below ducal rank are called lord and lady in speech, applies equally, of course, to viscounts and their wives. As in other ranks, there are a few formal occasions on which the full title would be used, but it would never happen in intimate speech.

Style of Addressing in Writing

The most formal manner is:

> My Lord,
> > I have the honour to remain,
> > > Your Lordship's obedient servant,

Address on envelope—
> The Right Hon. the Viscount O'Mara.

> Madam,
> > I have the honour to remain,
> > > Your Ladyship's obedient servant,

Address of envelope—
>The Right Hon. the Viscountess O'Mara.

Less formally, but still not socially:
>My Lord,
>>Yours faithfully,

Address of envelope—
>The Right Hon. the Viscount O'Mara.

>Madam,
>>Yours faithfully,

Address of envelope—
>The Right Hon. the Viscountess O'Mara.

The social manner of address in writing is:
>Dear Lord O'Mara,   *or*
>Dear O'Mara,
>>Yours sincerely,

Address of envelope—
>The Viscount O'Mara.

>Dear Lady O'Mara,
>>Yours sincerely,

Address of envelope—
>The Viscountess O'Mara.

Dowager Viscountesses

A dowager viscountess is the earliest surviving widow of a preceding peer (but *see* p. 39 for the Scottish practice). Later surviving widows are distinguished by the use of the Christian name before the title (*see* p. 39).

Style of Addressing in Speech

is exactly the same as if she were the reigning viscountess (*see above*).

Style of Addressing in Writing

The most formal manner is:

Madam,
            I have the honour to remain,
                        Your Ladyship's obedient servant,

Less formally:

Madam,
                        Yours faithfully,

Address of envelope—

The Right Hon. the Dowager Viscountess O'Mara,   *or*
The Right Hon. Anne, Viscountess O'Mara.

The social manner of address in writing is:

Dear Lady O'Mara,
                        Yours sincerely,

Address of envelope—

The Dowager Viscountess O'Mara,   *or*
Anne, Viscountess O'Mara.

The former wife of a Viscount uses her Christian name before the title.

Style of Addressing in Writing

The most formal manner is:

Madam,
            I have the honour to remain,
                        Your Ladyship's obedient servant,

Less formally:
>   Madam,
>   Yours faithfully,

> *Address of envelope*—
>   Anne, Viscountess O'Mara.

The social manner of address in writing is:
>   Dear Lady O'Mara,
>   Yours sincerely,

> *Address of envelope*—
>   Anne, Viscountess O'Mara.

Eldest Sons of Viscounts

Courtesy titles cease at the grade of an earl, so that the eldest son of a viscount does not take his father's second title, even if he happens to have one. Like his younger brothers, he is merely The Honourable, using his Christian name (not initials) and surname, and his wife shares the title.

> *Example.*—The Hon. Michael O'Mara.
> The Hon. Mrs Michael O'Mara.

Their visiting-cards would be inscribed "Mr O'Mara" and "Mrs O'Mara" without the Christian name.

Style of Addressing in Speech

As explained before, the title Honourable is never used in speech, so that the eldest son of our viscount would be spoken and referred to as Mr O'Mara and his wife as Mrs O'Mara. This rule is followed by servants also.

Style of Addressing in Writing

The most formal manner is:

Sir,

> I have the honour to remain,
> Your obedient servant,

Less formally:

Dear Sir,

> Yours faithfully,

Address of envelope—

The Hon. Michael O'Mara.

Madam,

> I have the honour to remain,
> Your obedient servant,

Less formally:

Dear Madam,

> Yours faithfully,

Address of envelope—

The Hon. Mrs Michael O'Mara.

The social manner of address in writing is:

Dear Mr O'Mara,

> Yours sincerely,

Address of envelope—

The Hon. Michael O'Mara.

Dear Mrs O'Mara,

> Yours sincerely,

Address of envelope—

The Hon. Mrs Michael O'Mara.

Widows of Eldest Sons of Viscounts

keep their title until re-marriage, when it is abandoned in favour
of the second husband's status, whether it be higher or lower.

This does not apply, of course, if the widow possesses a title in her own right. The same rules apply to former wives as to widows.

Younger Sons of Viscounts
Wives of Younger Sons of Viscounts
Widows of Younger Sons of Viscounts
Former Wives of Younger Sons of Viscounts

The same rules exactly apply here as to younger sons of earls and their wives (*see* pp. 73 and 74).

Daughters of Viscounts

all bear the title Honourable like their brothers.

Style of Addressing in Speech

The title is never used in speech even by a servant. The eldest daughter is referred to as Miss O'Mara, the younger ones as Miss Nora and Miss Bridget O'Mara.

Style of Addressing in Writing

is the same for all. The most formal manner is:

> Madam,
>> I have the honour to remain,
>>> Your obedient servant,

Less formally:

> Dear Madam,
>> Yours faithfully,

> *Address of envelope—*
>> The Hon. Eileen O'Mara.

The social manner of address in writing is:

> Dear Miss O'Mara,
>> Yours sincerely,

Address of envelope—
> The Hon. Eileen O'Mara.

Married Daughters of Viscounts

The daughter of a viscount, in marrying a man of lower rank than her own, keeps her title, thus:

Marriage with

A commoner	Mr Peter Green	The Hon. Mrs Green (not The Hon. Mrs Peter Green)
A knight or baronet	Sir Bernard Brown	The Hon. Lady Brown

In marrying a man of equal or higher rank she shares her husband's title.

Children of Sons of Viscounts
Children of Daughters of Viscounts

have no titles or distinctions of any sort. They have, of course, a certain social precedence.

BARONS AND BARONESSES

This is the fifth and last grade of the peerage. In England and Wales "Baron" and "Baroness" have always been the legal terms, whereas in Scotland the legal term for a hereditary peer of this rank whose title was created before 1707 is "Lord" or "Lady" (*see* PEERAGE OF SCOTLAND, p. 41). In usage, however, all of this rank are known as "Lord" or "Lady", with the exception of peeresses in their own right (including women life peers) who may choose to be called "Baroness".

The title is sometimes territorial, sometimes taken from the family name, and sometimes from other sources entirely.

Our example shall be Baron Westley, family name Whitworth.

Style of Addressing in Speech

The rule of addressing all peers below ducal rank as lord and lady is equally applicable to barons and their wives. Baronesses in their own right, however (including women life peers), are called The Baroness ———— if they so wish.

Style of Addressing in Writing

The most formal manner is:

> My Lord,
> > I have the honour to be,
> > > Your Lordship's obedient servant,

> *Address of envelope—*
> > The Right Hon. Lord Westley.

> Madam,
> > I have the honour to be,
> > > Your Ladyship's obedient servant,

Address of envelope—
> The Right Hon. Lady Westley.

Less formally, but still not socially:
> My Lord,
>> Yours faithfully,

Address of envelope—
> The Right Hon. Lord Westley.

> Madam,
>> Yours faithfully,

Address of envelope—
> The Right Hon. Lady Westley.

The social manner of address in writing is:
> Dear Lord Westley, *or*
> Dear Westley,
>> Yours sincerely,

Address of envelope—
> The Lord Westley.

> Dear Lady Westley,
>> Yours sincerely,

Address of envelope—
> The Lady Westley.

Dowager Baronesses

A dowager baroness is the earliest surviving widow of a preceding peer (but *see* p. 39 for the Scottish practice). Later surviving widows are distinguished by the use of the Christian name before the title (*see* p. 39).

Style of Addressing in Speech

is exactly the same as if she were the reigning baroness (*see* p. 86).

Style of Addressing in Writing

The most formal manner is:

Madam,

I have the honour to remain,
Your Ladyship's obedient servant,

Less formally:

Madam,

Yours faithfully,

Address of envelope—

The Right Hon. the Dowager Lady Westley, *or*
The Right Hon. Anne, Lady Westley.

The social manner of address in writing is:

Dear Lady Westley,
Yours sincerely,

Address of envelope—

The Dowager Lady Westley,   *or*
Anne, Lady Westley.

The former wife of a Baron uses her Christian name before the title.

Style of Addressing in Writing

The most formal manner is:

Madam,

I have the honour to remain,
Your Ladyship's obedient servant,

Less formally:
>   Madam,
>>   Yours faithfully,

>   *Address of envelope—*
>   Anne, Lady Westley.

The social manner of address in writing is:
>   Dear Lady Westley,
>>   Yours sincerely,

>   *Address of envelope—*
>   Anne, Lady Westley.

Eldest Sons of Barons

Courtesy titles cease at the grade of an earl, so that the eldest son of a baron, like his younger brothers, is merely The Honourable, and his wife shares the title. "The Honourable" is followed by a Christian name rather than initials.

>   *Example.*—The Hon. Roger Whitworth.
>   The Hon. Mrs Roger Whitworth.

Their visiting-cards would be inscribed Mr Whitworth and Mrs Whitworth, without the Christian name.

Style of Addressing in Speech

As explained elsewhere, the title Honourable is never used in speech, so that the eldest son of our baron would be spoken and referred to as Mr Whitworth and his wife as Mrs Whitworth. This rule is followed by servants also.

Style of Addressing in Writing

The most formal manner is:

Sir,

I have the honour to remain,
Your obedient servant,

Less formally:

Dear Sir,

Yours faithfully,

Address of envelope—
The Hon. Roger Whitworth.

Madam,

I have the honour to remain,
Your obedient servant,

Less formally:

Dear Madam,

Yours faithfully,

Address of envelope—
The Hon. Mrs Roger Whitworth.

The social manner of address in writing is:

Dear Mr Whitworth,

Yours sincerely,

Address of envelope—

The Hon. Roger Whitworth.

Dear Mrs Whitworth,

Yours sincerely,

Address of envelope—

The Hon. Mrs Roger Whitworth.

Widows of Eldest Sons of Barons

keep their title until re-marriage, when it is abandoned in favour
of the second husband's status, whether it be higher or lower.
This does not apply, of course, if the widow possesses a title in her
own right. The same rules apply to former wives as to widows.

Younger Sons of Barons
Wives of Younger Sons of Barons
Widows of Younger Sons of Barons
Former Wives of Younger Sons of Barons

The same rules exactly apply here as to younger sons of earls and
their wives (*see* pp. 73 and 74).

Daughters of Barons

all bear the title of Honourable, and the same rules apply as for
daughters of viscounts (*see* p. 82).

Married Daughters of Barons

The daughter of a baron, in marrying a man of lower rank than
her own, keeps her title, thus:

Marriage with

A commoner	Mr Peter Green	The Hon. Mrs Green (not The Hon. Mrs Peter Green)
A knight or baronet	Sir Bernard Brown	The Hon. Lady Brown

In marrying a man of equal or higher rank she shares her
husband's title.

Children of Sons of Barons
Children of Daughters of Barons

have no titles or distinctions of any sort.

MALTESE NOBILITY

Maltese titles are Marquis, Count and Baron; the head of the family in each case is addressed as The Most Noble, followed by the title, and the heir as Marchesino, Contino or Baroncino —————; other sons and daughters are addressed The Noble, with Christian name and title.

BARONETS

This title, identified by the prefix Sir to Christian and surname, is a hereditary honour descending from father to son. Failing a son to the first holder, the title becomes extinct; but failing a son to a later holder, the title goes to the nearest male descendant of a former holder. It is distinguished from that of knight by the word baronet, or one of its contractions, being added at the end of the name, thus:

Sir George Robinson, Bt.

Where a Scottish family uses a territorial title this is inserted before the addition "Bt.".

Sir George Robinson of Glenrobinson, Bt.

The word baronet is used in full only in formal documents. Bt. is the older abbreviation and the only one recognized by the Council of the Baronetage, but, in spite of this, Bart. is still much used. This is a pity, because it is considered wrong by those who know and prefer the right way.

A baronet's wife takes the title of Lady in conjunction with the surname only—never with her own or her husband's Christian name unless she happens to have a title of her own (*see* pp. 46, 57, 66, 76, 83, and 89).

Example.—Lady Robinson.

She is not entitled to be called The Lady Robinson (*see* p. 46).

The only exception to this rule might be the written one of Lady (George) Robinson, when it is necessary to distinguish her from another Lady Robinson. In actual speech there can be no such distinction. In Scotland, however, the territorial addition (if it exists) acts as the distinction:

Lady Robinson of Glenrobinson.

Style of Addressing in Speech

A baronet is addressed by his title and Christian name, as, for instance, Sir George, and spoken of as Sir George Robinson, or, more familiarly, as Sir George. There is no distinction here between a baronet and a knight.

Style of Addressing in Writing

The most formal manner is:

> Sir,
>
> > I have the honour to remain,
> > > Your obedient servant,

Less formally, but still not socially:

> Dear Sir,
>
> > Yours faithfully,

Address of envelope—

> Sir George Robinson, Bt.
> Sir George Robinson of Glenrobinson, Bt.

> Madam,
>
> > I have the honour to remain,
> > > Your Ladyship's obedient servant,

Less formally, but still not socially:

> Dear Madam,
>
> > Yours faithfully,

Address of envelope—

> Lady Robinson.
> Lady Robinson of Glenrobinson.

The social manner of address in writing is:

> Dear Sir George Robinson,
> > Yours sincerely,

or more familiarly

Dear Sir George,
                        Yours sincerely,

Address of envelope—
        Sir George Robinson, Bt.

Dear Lady Robinson,
                        Yours sincerely,

Address of envelope—
        Lady Robinson.

Baronetess

There are very few baronetcies (all of them are Scottish) where it is possible for a lady to inherit the title. Only one is at present held by a lady. She is addressed in the same way as a baronet's wife; but where for a baronet the abbreviation Bt. would be added, her name should be followed by Btss.

Address of envelope—
        Lady Robinson of Glenrobinson, Btss.

Widows of Baronets

retain their style of address unless and until the succeeding baronet marries, when the widow is called either

                The Dowager Lady Robinson,   *or*
                Dora, Lady Robinson.

The rule follows that of the peerage (*see* p. 39).

Style of Addressing in Speech

is the same as for a baronet's wife(*see* p. 92).

Style of Addressing in Writing

The most formal manner is:

> Madam,
>> I have the honour to remain,
>>> Your Ladyship's obedient servant,

Less formally:

> Dear Madam,
>> Yours faithfully,

Address of envelope—

> The Dowager Lady Robinson,   *or*
> Dora, Lady Robinson.

The social manner of address in writing is:

> Dear Lady Robinson,
>> Yours sincerely,

Address of envelope—

> The Dowager Lady Robinson,   *or*
> Dora, Lady Robinson.

Widows of Baronets Re-marrying

If marrying a peer, an honourable, or another baronet, the title and name of the new husband is taken. If she marries an untitled gentleman, she becomes Mrs ————.

Former Wives of Baronets

Until remarriage they are addressed in the same way as widows, except that they will not be Dowager, but will use a Christian name before the title.

Children of Baronets

have no titles or distinctions, excepting that the eldest son's Christian name is not used.

>   *Example.*—Mr Robinson.

In Scottish families which have a territorial designation (see p. 106), he is styled "younger" (which may be abbreviated yr.) of the family description.

>   *Example.*—Mr Robinson, younger of Glenrobinson.

Honourables

When the son of a viscount or baron, or the younger son of an earl, receives a baronetcy, the foregoing rules apply, excepting as to the address of envelopes, which should be:

>   The Hon. Sir George Robinson, Bt.
>   The Hon. Lady Robinson.

KNIGHTS

The first rule for all knights who have no other title is that they are addressed as Sir, with one Christian name and surname (Sir James Brown), and that their wives are addressed as Lady, with the surname alone (Lady Brown). The orders of knighthood are various, but not one of them is hereditary. We will take them in the order of their precedence and deal with general rules as they arise.

The Most Noble Order of the Garter

This order is conferred most often, but not exclusively, upon royalties and in the peerage. It is distinguished by the letters K.G. after the name and title:

> *Example.*—The Duke of Middlesex, K.G.

The Most Ancient and Most Noble Order of the Thistle

This order is conferred exclusively upon Scottish nobles (these include both peers and certain commoners as nobles in the technical sense) and is distinguished by the letters K.T. after the name and title.

> *Example.*—The Earl of Queensferry, K.T.
> Sir William MacHector of Drimmore, K.T.

The Most Illustrious Order of St. Patrick

This order was conferred exclusively upon Irish nobles, and distinguished by the letters K.P. after the name and title.

> *Example.*—The Viscount O'Mara, K.P.

No appointments have been made to the order since 1922.

The Most Honourable Order of the Bath

This is the first of the orders of knighthood in which there is more than one class. Women as well as men are eligible. Members of the first two classes only are knights, and the use of the title in speech and writing is the same as for baronets and their wives and children (except, of course, for the abbreviation Bt.).

The classes and distinctions, for men, are as follows:

Knights Grand Cross	Sir Robert Johnson, G.C.B.
Knights Commanders	Sir Edward Thompson, K.C.B.
Companions	Richard Jackson, Esq., C.B.

The wives of companions, as such, have no distinctions, though they have recognized precedence. The classes for women are:

Dames Grand Cross	Dame Matilda Johnson, G.C.B.
Dames Commanders	Dame Pamela Thompson, D.C.B.
Companions	Mrs Jackson, C.B.

Husbands of ladies raised to any one of the ranks in this order do not share their wives' distinctions.

The title carried by the first two degrees of this order is used always in conjunction with the lady's Christian name. The formal mode of address in speech is "Dame Matilda" or "Dame Pamela". The most formal address in writing is:

> Madam,
>> I beg to remain,
>>> Your obedient servant,

Less formally:

> Dear Madam,
>> Yours faithfully,

The social manner of address in writing is:

> Dear Dame Matilda Johnson,   *or*
> Dear Dame Matilda,
>> Yours sincerely,

Address of envelope—
> Dame Matilda Johnson, G.C.B. (or D.C.B.).

Where the recipient of this honour already enjoys a higher title, either by birth or marriage, the accepted rule would seem to be that for a peeress, or the daughter of a duke, marquess, or earl, her title in this order is indicated only the letters following her name; that the prefix "The Hon." should be used with and preceding "Dame" (as with a knight); and that the wives or widows of baronets and knights may themselves choose whether they wish to be known as, e.g., Lady Jones, D.C.B., or Dame Bronwen Jones, D.C.B.

The Most Exalted Order of the Star of India

As in the previous case, this order (which is no longer conferred) has three classes. Members of the first two classes only are knights, and the use of the title in speech and writing is the same as for baronets and their wives and children (excepting, of course, the abbreviation Bt.).

Knights Grand Commanders	Sir Robert Johnson, G.C.S.I.
Knights Commanders	Sir Edward Thompson, K.C.S.I.
Companions	Richard Jackson, Esq., C.S.I.

The wives of companions, as such, have no distinctions, though they have recognized precedence.

The Most Distinguished Order of St. Michael and St. George

There are three classes in this order, for which women as well as men are eligible:

Knights Grand Cross	Sir Robert Johnson, G.C.M.G.
Knights Commanders	Sir Edward Thompson, K.C.M.G.
Companions	Richard Jackson, Esq., C.M.G.

Members of the first two classes only are knights, and the use of the title in speech and writing is the same as for baronets and their wives and children (except, of course, for the abbreviation Bt.). The wives of companions, as such, have no distinctions, though they have recognized precedence.

The three classes for women are:

Dames Grand Cross	Dame Matilda Johnson, G.C.M.G.
Dames Commanders	Dame Pamela Thompson, D.C.M.G.
Companions	Mrs Jackson, C.M.G.

Husbands of ladies raised to any one of the ranks in this order do not share their wives' distinctions.

The title carried by the first two degrees of this order is used always in conjunction with the lady's Christian name. The formal mode of address in speech is "Dame Matilda" or "Dame Pamela". The most formal mode of address in writing is:

Madam,
I beg to remain,
Your obedient servant,

Less formally:

Dear Madam,
Yours faithfully,

The social manner of address in writing is:

Dear Dame Matilda Johnson, *or* Dear Dame Matilda,
Yours sincerely,

Address of envelope—
Dame Matilda Johnson, G.C.M.G. (or D.C.M.G.)

The use of the title carried by the first two degrees of this order (except, of course, that the letters after the name are G.C.M.G. or D.C.M.G.) is the same as for the Order of the Bath (*see* p. 98).

The Most Eminent Order of the Indian Empire

There are three classes in this order (which is no longer confer-red), member of the first two classes only being knights. The use of the title in speech and writing is the same as for baronets and their wives and children (excepting, of course, the abbreviation Bt.). The wives of companions, as such, have no distinctions, though they have recognized precedence.

Knights Grand	
Commanders	Sir Robert Johnson, G.C.I.E.
Knights Commanders	Sir Edward Thompson, K.C.I.E.
Companions	Richard Jackson, Esq., C.I.E.

The Royal Victorian Order

There are five classes in this order, for which women as well as men are eligible:

Knights Grand Cross	Sir Robert Johnson, G.C.V.O.
Knights Commanders	Sir Edward Thompson, K.C.V.O.
Commanders	Richard Jackson, Esq., C.V.O.
Members Fourth Class	Herbert Black, Esq., M.V.O.
Members Fifth Class	Charles White, Esq., M.V.O.

Members of the first two classes only are knights, and the use of the title in speech and writing (except, of course, for the abbreviation Bt.) is the same as for baronets and their wives and children. The wives of commanders and members, as such, have no distinctions, though they have recognized precedence.

The five classes for women are:

Dames Grand Cross	Dame Matilda Johnson, G.C.V.O.
Dames Commanders	Dame Pamela Thompson, D.C.V.O.
Commanders	Mrs Jackson, C.V.O.
Members Fourth Class	Mrs Black, M.V.O.
Members Fifth Class	Miss Brown, M.V.O.

Husbands of ladies raised to any one of the ranks in this order do not share their wives' distinctions.

The use of the title carried by the first two degrees of this order (except, of course, that the letters after the name are G.C.V.O. or D.C.V.O.) is the same as for the Order of the Bath (*see* p. 98).

The Most Excellent Order of the British Empire

This order is the most recent, and women as well as men are eligible. The five classes for men are:

Knights Grand Cross	Sir Robert Johnson, G.B.E.
Knights Commanders	Sir Edward Thompson, K.B.E.
Commanders	Richard Jackson, Esq., C.B.E.
Officers	Herbert Black, Esq., O.B.E.
Members	Thomas Brown, Esq., M.B.E.

Members of the first two classes only are knights, and the use of the title in speech and writing (except, of course, the abbreviation Bt.) is the same as for baronets and their wives and children. The wives of commanders, officers, and members, as such, have no distinctions, though they have recognized precedence.

The five classes for women are:

Dames Grand Cross	Dame Matilda Johnson, G.B.E.
Dames Commanders	Dame Pamela Thompson, D.B.E.
Commanders	Mrs Jackson, C.B.E.
Officers	Mrs Black, O.B.E.
Members	Miss Brown, M.B.E.

Husbands of ladies raised to any one of the ranks in this order do not share their wives' distinctions.

The use of the title carried by the first two degrees of this order (except, of course, that the letters after the name are G.B.E. or D.B.E.) is the same as for the Order of the Bath (*see* p. 98).

Knights Bachelor

This is the lowest order of knighthood, and is designated thus:

Sir William Jones,

this is, with Christian name (not initials) and surname preceded by the title Sir.

Only in formal documents is the word Knight or the abbreviation Kt. sometimes added to the name. It is never correct to use the letters K.B. to signify a Knight Bachelor. In all other respects the use of the title in speech and writing (except, of course, the abbreviation Bt.) is the same as for baronets and their wives and children (*see* pp. 92 to 96).

Widows of Knights

No change is made; they continue to be known as Lady ————.

Widows of Knights Re-marrying

See under BARONETS (p. 95).

Honorary Orders of Knighthood

These are conferred from time to time on foreigners. Except in rare cases granted specially by the Sovereign, the recipient has no right to the title of Sir and it should not be used before the name; but the letters signifying membership of an order may be used after the name, without the abbreviation Hon., e.g.

Mr Albert C. Gould, K.B.E.

New Titles (Knights and Dames)

All persons awarded Orders, decorations, and medals may add the appropriate letters to their names immediately after the announcement in the *London Gazette*, e.g.:

> John Smith, Esq., C.B.E.
> Major Evan Jones, M.C.
> Corporal William Brown, M.M.

Knights Grand Cross and Knights Commanders of Orders of Chivalry and Knights Bachelor may use the prefix "Sir" immediately after the official announcement in the *London Gazette*.

A Knight's appointment is completed when he receives the accolade from the Sovereign. In very rare cases, where personal investiture is impracticable, Letters Patent granting full privileges of the honour are issued.

Ladies who are appointed Dames Grand Cross or Dames Commanders of Orders of Chivalry may assume the prefix "Dame" as soon as the notice appears in the *London Gazette*. (*See* p. 43 for new peerages.)

General Remarks

All the letters signifying membership of orders, and all decorations, should be used in addressing, subject to the point made below, that a lower rank in an order is absorbed in a higher. These letters are shown in the correct order on p. 179.

In the case of a Knight Bachelor being also a companion in another order, his designation would be:

> Sir Henry Jones, C.B.

In this case the letters K.C.B. would be wrong, because, although a knight and a member of the Order of the Bath, he is not a knight in that particular order.

When a member of an order of knighthood is promoted to a higher rank within the same order, the lower rank is absorbed in the higher and therefore the designation of the lower rank is omitted after the name. Thus when Richard Jackson, Esq., C.V.O., is created a knight of the Royal Victorian Order he becomes Sir Richard Jackson, K.C.V.O.

When the son of a viscount or baron or the younger son of an earl receives a knighthood, the foregoing rules apply, excepting as to the address of envelopes, which should be:

The Hon. Sir William Browning, K.C.M.G. (or otherwise).
The Hon. Lady Browning.

Knighthoods in Orders not Bestowed by the Crown

Although appointments in the Most Venerable Order of the Hospital of St John of Jerusalem are gazetted, knights and dames in the order do not receive the accolade, nor are they addressed as Sir or Dame. The letters G.C.St.J., K.St.J. and D.St.J. are not used after the name. Papal knighthoods in the orders of St Gregory the Great and St Sylvester also do not confer titles, nor do knighthoods in the Sovereign Military Order of Malta; the abbreviations sometimes seen (G.C.S.G., K.S.G., K.S.S., K.M., for example) should equally not be used after the name.

CHIEFS OF SCOTTISH CLANS
AND TERRITORIAL HOUSES (LAIRDS)

By Scots Law and custom Chiefs of Scottish Clans and Names, chieftains, and lairds are known by chiefly styles or territorial designations which are legally part of their surnames. Mr is not used, and Esq. seldom. Mackvicular of Mackvicular is called Mackvicular in his own territorial district or gathering, and elsewhere The Mackvicular—if he be chief of a *whole* "Name" or "clan" (The Armstrength, and The Mackvicular, are not translations of the Gaelic *An*, but a 15-century Scots style). MacHector of Drimmore is called Drimmore.

The style of address in speech is Mackvicular, or Drimmore, *without* Mr—whatever the rank of the speaker.

The normal mode of address in writing is Sir (or Dear Sir)—but a clansman would write Dear Chief.

The social mode of address is:

> Dear Mackvicular, *or* Dear Drimmore.

The addresss of envelopes has varied, but since most chiefs were feudal Barons (who had precedence of ordinary Esquires), the tendency is, again, to omit Esq., and frequently Christian name, thus:

> The Mackvicular of Mackvicular,
> MacHector of Drimmore, *or*
> John Brown of Frenchie.

English writers who feel uneasy at the omission of Esq. may use it; in this case it *follows* the clan or territorial designation.

Where the chief or laird is a baronet or a knight he is called, for example,

> Sir James MacHector of Drimmore;

106

service rank is used in the usual way:

> Colonel The Mackvicular, D.S.O.

Any decorations follow the territorial designation.
Their wives are addressed formally in writing as:

Madam (or Dear Madam),

and socially as:

> Dear Mrs Mackvicular of Mackvicular,   *or*
> Dear Mrs MacHector of Drimmore,

They are introduced or announced as:

> Mrs Mackvicular of Mackvicular,   *or*
> Mrs MacHector of Drimmore.

Their heirs are addressed in writing with the distinction 'younger', often abbreviated to 'yr.', before or after the territorial designation, as:

> John Mackvicular, younger of Mackvicular,   *or*
> James MacHector of Drimmore, younger,

and they are also introduced or announced in this way.
   All unmarried daughters use the title, thus:

> Miss MacHector of Drimmore—for the eldest, and
> Miss Jean MacHector of Drimmore—for a younger one.

It is not the custom for younger sons to use the title.
   The old Scottish title of "Laird" is still freely used in Scotland, and even a landless chief can be styled in writing, or referred to in speech, as The Laird of Mackvicular, and any other proprietor is styled, e.g. The Laird of Drimmore.

Their wives are in rural Scotland still styled (and legally so, if the wife of a chief, or feudal baron) as:

> The Lady Mackvicular,   *or*   The Lady Drimmore.

Southern Society deprecated (whilst local custom retained)

these titles, and "Mrs" (which has a different origin) was introduced from England towards the close of the 18th century. Technically the "Madam" retained by wives of Irish Chieftains is correct, and a few Scottish ones now use it.

The widow of a Chief or Laird continues to use the territorial style and the prefix Dowager may be used in the same circumstances as where it is applied to a Peeress (*see* p. 39):

The Dowager Mrs Mackvicular of Mackvicular.

IRISH CHIEFTAINS

Under the Brehon Law, the succession of Irish chieftains was by selection within a limited family group (*deirbhfine*), but the principle of seniority was observed by Gaelic genealogists. About the beginning of the 19th century some of the representatives of the last holders of the chieftainries resumed the appropriate designations, which had lapsed with the destruction of the Gaelic order.

The descent of the following by primogeniture in the male line from the last inaugurated or *de facto* chieftain has been examined by the Genealogical Office, Dublin Castle. Subject to the possible survival in some cases of senior lines at present unidentified, they are recorded at the Genealogical Office as Chiefs of the Name and are recognized by courtesy. Certain chiefs whose pedigrees have not been finally proved are included in this list on account of their prescriptive standing.

> Mac Dermot Prince of Coolavin.
> Mac Gillycuddy of the Reeks.
> Mac Murrough Kavanagh.
> O Brien of Thomond.
> O Callaghan.
> O Conor Don.
> O Donel of Tirconnell.
> O Donoghue of the Glens.
> O Donovan.
> O Morchoe.
> O Neill of Clandeboy.
> O Sionnaigh (called The Fox since 1552).
> O Toole of Fer Tire.
> O Grady of Kilballyowen.
> O Kelly of Gallagh and Tycooly.

The address on the envelope is as the above designation (e.g. O Donoghue of the Glens), or with the prefix "The", which although not officially recognized is generally used (e.g. The Mac Dermot). The social mode of address is "Dear O Donoghue", etc.

There are three knights of a palatine creation by an Earl of Desmond in the 14th century, the Knight of Glin, the Knight of Kerry, and the White Knight (this last title is dormant). They are so designated, and so addressed on the envelope.

The social mode of address is "Dear Knight of Glin", etc.

The wives of persons designated chieftains are addressed as "Madam O Donoghue", etc. The wives of the knights palatine are addressed as the wives of chieftains (but the Knight of Kerry is a baronet, and his wife should be addressed as a baronet's wife).

The sons and daughters are addressed as the children of an Esquire.

ESQUIRES

The use of this title for every man who cannot claim a higher one persists, far more widely than used to be the case, when social usage limited its application to those considered to merit it through social standing, membership of one of the professions, possession of a degree from Oxford or Cambridge University, and so on. It is felt to be more courteous in general to use it in all correspondence, although a reaction, influenced by usage in the United States and some other English-speaking countries, now leads many writers, especially in business, to prefer the use of Mr. Whichever style is preferred, it should clearly be used consistently, since the difficulty of ascertaining which of one's correspondents is *entitled* to the appellation Esquire must rule out any thought of using it only where it was, in the past, conferred by social position or other qualification. It should, however, not be used in addressing Quakers, who dislike the form.

The title Esquire should never be used in conjunction with any other title, as for instance the prefix Mr. Some doubt arises occasionally as to the lesser grades of orders of knighthood. Commanders, Companions, Officers and Members of the various orders of knighthood are addressed as esquires with the distinguishing abbreviation after the name, thus:

Richard Jackson, Esq., C.V.O.

(For fuller details *see under* KNIGHTS, p. 97.)

This being so, the following are the correct uses for the head of the family. The formal manner of address in speech is Sir, and the social manner Mr Robins. His wife is called Madam, and referred to as Mrs Robins. The most formal manner of address in writing is:

111

Sir,

          I beg to remain, Sir,
                    Your obedient servant,

Madam,

          I beg to remain, Madam,
                    Your obedient servant,

Less formally, but still not socially:

Dear Sir,

                    Yours faithfully,

Dear Madam,

                    Yours faithfully,

The social manner of address in writing is:

Dear Mr Robins,

                    Yours sincerely,

Dear Mrs Robins,

                    Yours sincerely,

Address on enveloples—

        Harold Robins, Esq., or H. J. Robins, Esq.,
        Mrs Robins, Mrs Harold Robins, or Mrs H. J. Robins.

(If the person concerned has two or more forenames, it is preferable to use initials; if one only, the name in full.)

For all other male members of the family the rules are the same, but envelopes to their wives always include their husbands' Christian names, for instance:

Mrs John Robins.

Wives of commoners take precedence in the family from their husbands, as in the titled classes. Once a woman marries the head of the family, or the man who subsequently becomes the head of the family, this position remains with her for life, unless she re-marries or the marriage is dissolved.

It is wrong to change the form of address on widowhood; Mrs John Robins remains Mrs John Robins when her husband dies, and should not be addressed by her own Christian name. This error might moreover lead strangers to suppose that her marriage had been dissolved; a former wife would normally use her own Christian name or initials, thus:

> Mrs Mary Robins.
> Mrs M. A. Robins.

Sons

bearing the same name or initials as their fathers may be addressed:

> Harold Robins, Jnr., Esq.,

if this is necessary to avoid confusion.

There was a Victorian habit of addressing young men of nursery and school age as Master Robins, which seems happily to be dying out. Now the more sensible manner of addressing all boys is simply Harold Robins, until they are grown up and worthy of the title Esq.

Daughters

The eldest unmarried daughter of the head of the family is Miss Robins. All other unmarried women in the family use their distinguishing Christian names, for example:

> Miss Jane Robins.

DOUBLE NAMES

The justification for a hyphenated double name is when two land-owning families have been merged into one through marriage, or when legal licence to adopt it has been obtained. The form need not be denied, however, to those who use a second Christian name prefixed to the surname for distinction or for convenience, though in such cases a hyphen should not be used. In speech as well as writing the two names are always used.

Joint Forms of Address

It is occasionally necessary to address a letter to husband and wife jointly, although this should be avoided if possible. The only difficulty arises where each spouse is entitled to a different form of address; on these occasions it is necessary to distinguish between them:

> Mr and Mrs R. F. Jackson.
> The Lord and Lady Jackson.
> *but* The Revd. R. F. and Mrs Jackson.
> Sir Richard and Lady Jackson.
> Mr R. F. and the Hon. Mrs Jackson.
> Sir Richard Jackson, Bt., and Lady Jackson.

Where one spouse has honours or decorations indicated by letters after the name these must be shown with the right name:

> Colonel R. F. Jackson, C.B.E., and Mrs Jackson.
> Sir Richard Jackson and Dame Patricia Jackson, D.B.E.
> Mr R. F. Jackson and Dame Mary Jackson, D.C.M.G.
> Sir Richard Jackson, K.B.E., and Lady Jackson.

PRESIDENTS OF SOCIETIES

The presidents of societies are addressed in formal speech and writing as Sir or Mr President. In the case of a titled holder of the office he would be addressed according to his rank, e.g. My Lord Duke (or Your Grace) and President, or My Lord and President, etc. Where a woman holds office she is addressed as Madam President (except that a duchess would be Your Grace and President). In all cases envelopes are addressed according to name and rank, with the addition of

President of The —————.

PRIVY COUNSELLORS

This office is conferred for life, but it is not hereditary. All members of the Cabinet must be privy counsellors, but all privy counsellors are not members of the Cabinet. Women as well as men may be appointed privy counsellors.

There is nothing to indicate this rank in the style of addressing in speech, which is according to the holder's rank otherwise, but in writing the name is preceded with the distinction The Right Hon. Wives do not share this title. In the case of the peerage the office of privy counsellor is not indicated, as in the three lowest grades the title of Right Hon. is already used and in the two highest grades it is assumed to be incorporated in the loftier titles (*see* p. 46).

Examples are as follows: A commoner is referred and spoken to as Mr Williams, while the manner of address in writing is, formally,

> Sir (or Dear Sir),
> > I have the honour to be, Sir (or Dear Sir),
> > > Yours faithfully,

Less formally:

> Dear Sir,
> > Yours faithfully,

Or socially:

> Dear Mr Williams,
> > Yours sincerely,

Address of envelope in all cases—
> The Right Hon. James Williams.

Esq. is not used, nor are initials, but Christian name and surname.

His wife does not share the title, and would therefore always be addressed in speech and writing as Mrs Williams.

A lady who is appointed privy counsellor is referred and spoken to as Mrs Matilda Johnson, while the formal manner of address in writing is: The Right Hon. Matilda Johnson, omitting Mrs or Miss. Husbands of ladies appointed privy counsellors do not share this title.

In the case of Navy, Army or Air Force officers the style of address in writing is, for example,

Admiral The Right Hon. Sir James Smith

or

Colonel The Right Hon. Henry Jones

or

Air Vice-Marshal The Right Hon. Sir Josiah Blank.

In the case of Church dignitaries the style of address in writing would be, for example,

The Most Revd. and Right Hon. the Lord Archbishop of Blank.

The Right Revd. and Right Hon. the Lord Bishop of Blank.

ECCLESIASTICAL

The Church of England

Lords Spiritual

The Archbishops of Canterbury and York, the Bishops of London, Durham, and Winchester, and twenty-one of the other English Diocesan Bishops in order of seniority constitute the Lords Spiritual in Parliament. The Bishop of Sodor and Man is not summoned.

Archbishops

The Archbishop of Canterbury ranks next in precedence to the Royal Family, and above dukes in the Roll of Peerage. The Archbishop of York ranks next to the Lord Chancellor.

Style of Addressing in Speech

The manner of addressing the Archbishops of Canterbury and York in speech both by equals and inferiors is "Your Grace". They are referred to by their territorial titles, e.g. The Archbishop of Canterbury, and not by name; but where no confusion is likely, "the Archbishop" is sufficient. Only past or retired prelates are referred to by name, e.g. Archbishop Temple.

Style of Addressing in Writing

The most formal manner is:

> My Lord Archbishop, *or*
> Your Grace,
>
>> I have the honour to remain, my Lord Archbishop,
>> Your Grace's devoted and obedient servant,

Less formally:

>My Lord Archbishop,
>>Yours faithfully,

The Archbishops of Canterbury and York, being Privy Counsellors, are addressed on the envelope as:

>>The Most Revd. and Right Hon. the Lord Archbishop of Canterbury (or York).

Other Archbishops are addressed on the envelope, both formally and socially, as:

>>The Most Revd. the Lord Archbishop of —————.

The social manner of address in writing is:

>Dear Lord Archbishop, *or*
>Dear Archbishop,
>>Yours sincerely,

The same modes of address are applicable to all Archbishops of the Anglican Communion in accordance with the general principles set out below (*see* BISHOPS, p. 121). An exception, however, occurs in the case of the Archbishop of Armagh, who is addressed thus:

>The Most Revd. His Grace the Lord Primate of all Ireland.

Signatures

A reigning archbishop uses his Christian name in English or Latin, or the initials of his Christian names, coupled with the Latin name of his see, or some abbreviation of it (when the abbreviated Latin name of the see is used it is usual to put a colon instead of a full stop). The Archbishop of Canterbury signs himself (*e.g.* Thomas) Cantuar:, and the Archbishop of York signs (*e.g.* Henry) Ebor:.

Wives of Archbishops

The wife of an archbishop does not share her husband's precedence unless, of course, he possesses a temporal title as well as the spiritual one, in which case rules previously given would apply. Otherwise she is plain Mrs.

Retired Archbishops

On resigning, an archbishop, though relinquishing his legal, constitutional and ecclesiastical status as archbishop, remains a bishop, and should in principle be addressed as Right Reverend rather than Most Reverend. By courtesy, nevertheless (or by habit), he may still be addressed as archbishop; unless having perhaps held archiespiscopal office overseas, he should be appointed a bishop in this country, when he will be addressed as a bishop. This will be so if the appointment be as diocesan, suffragan or assistant bishop, according to the rule for each.

It has recently been the custom to bestow a temporal peerage upon a retiring Archbishop of Canterbury, who would otherwise renounce his seat in the House of Lords. The most formal manner of address in such cases is:

> My Lord,   *or*
> My Lord Archbishop (where this form of address is retained).
> I have the honour to remain, My Lord (or My Lord
> Archbishop),
> Your devoted and obedient servant,

Address of envelope—

> The Rt. Revd. and Rt. Hon. Lord ————,   *or*
> The Most Revd. and Rt. Hon. Lord ————.

As a Privy Counsellor, he retains the address Rt. Hon.

In all other cases the formal manner of address is the same, except for the mode of address on the envelope which should be:

Address of envelope—

> The Most Revd. John Brown.
> The Rt. Revd. John Brown.

There is no alternative to discovering which form is preferred in each case.

Retired Archbishops are addressed and referred to in speech, both socially and formally, by title and surname; it is again necessary to discover whether Archbishop, or Bishop, is preferred.

Example.—Archbishop Brown, *or* Archbishop Lord Lang.

They use their ordinary signatures, with the addition of Archbishop or Bishop.

Bishops

It is common knowledge that the title "Lord Bishop" is not confined to those English diocesan bishops who happen by reason of seniority to have seats in the House of Lords. All diocesan bishops of England are described in legal documents as Lord Bishops. Nor can the title be traced to the fact that bishops were formerly barons also, possessing land and revenues accordingly. The title *Dominus Episcopus* was in use before the Conquest and before the bishops were constituted barons.

All the bishops of the Anglican Communion have come by custom or right to be styled Lord Bishops. The title owes nothing to special grant or to any act of sovereignty by monarch. From time immemorial the Episcopal character and office have attracted forms of address of the highest dignity and reverence. Their variable forms have taken their present shape of Lord Bishop, a title which may be used with propriety of all episcopally consecrated bishops. Though in the Eastern churches titles more splendid and picturesque are in use, Lord Bishop is never wrong.

Among bishops of the Anglican Communion there are some in Missionary sees who modestly discourage the use of the title.

Until lately it has been unknown in the American Episcopal Church, so far as domestic use is concerned, but American bishops should in courtesy be addressed by English-speaking correspondents outside the U.S.A. in the manner applicable to all other bishops of the Anglican Communion. The American style "Right Reverend Sir" is, indeed, giving place occasionally to "My Lord" in U.S.A.

The twenty-four English bishops who, with the two archbishops, have seats in the House of Lords, rank below viscounts and above barons. The manner of address in speech is My Lord and His Lordship, both formally and socially.

The most formal manner of address in writing is:

> My Lord,   *or*
> My Lord Bishop,
> > I have the honour to remain,
> > > Your Lordship's obedient servant,

Less formally, but still not socially:

> My Lord,
> > Yours faithfully,

The social manner of address is:

> Dear Lord Bishop,   *or*   Dear Bishop,
> > Yours sincerely,

> *Address of envelope in all cases—*
> > The Right Revd. the Lord Bishop of ————.

Bishops Suffragan

In the United Kingdom they are not addressed as such but by courtesy exactly as diocesan bishops; they are styled Bishop of ————, not Bishop Suffragan of whatever the diocese may be. (The Bishops Suffragan of Grantham and Grimsby are addressed as though they were diocesan bishops of sees of these names, and not as Bishops Suffragan in the diocese of Lincoln.) In Canada and Australia, however, although they may (particularly in Canada) be given a territorial style of their own, they are thought of and addressed as suffragans of the diocese:

The Right Revd. the Suffragan Bishop of —————.

Bishops of the Anglican Communion

The manner of address in speech and writing, both formally and socially, is exactly the same as for English bishops. There are, however, the following minor points of distinction to be borne in mind.

Irish Bishops

The manner of address in speech and writing is the same as for English bishops.

The exception is the Bishop of Meath, who is addressed as "The Most Revd." instead of "The Right Revd.", as Premier Bishop of the Church of Ireland.

Scottish Bishops

The same as for Irish bishops (*see above*). The Primus is addressed in speech and writing as "My Lord" or "My Lord Primus".

Address of envelope—

The Most Revd. the Primus.

Bishops Coadjutor

In the Anglican church overseas Bishops Coadjutor may be appointed to assist an Archbishop. They have no separate territorial style, and are addressed by name, with the addition of their office:

The Right Revd. A. B. —————,
Bishop Coadjutor of —————.

Assistant Bishops

In Britain Assistant Bishops may be appointed, after retirement as a diocesan or suffragan, to assist the bishop of the diocese in which they are living. They are addressed by name. In the Anglican church overseas this title may be given to younger men who after consecration are appointed to assist the bishop of a large diocese. The form of address is the same in either case:

The Right Revd. C.D. ————.

Retired Bishops

Retired bishops are addressed by their names, but otherwise as for English bishops:

Example.—Dear Lord Bishop, *or* Dear Bishop, *and envelopes should be addressed—*

The Right Revd. John Brown.

Wives of Bishops
(Rules as for ARCHBISHOPS, p. 120.)

Deans

are addressed in speech as Mr Dean or Dean. The most formal manner of address in writing is:

Very Reverend Sir,
              I have the honour to remain, Very Reverend Sir,
                         Your obedient servant,

Less formally, but not socially or on a church matter:

Dear Sir,

Yours faithfully,

The social manner of address in writing is:

Dear Mr Dean,   *or*
Dear Dean,

Yours sincerely,

Address of envelope—

> The Very Revd. the Dean of ————.

Deans who are also Bishops are addressed as The Right Revd. the Dean of ————.

Retired Deans

have no right to the title on retirement, and are addressed as other members of the clergy (*see* p. 128), but if the title Dean Emeritus is conferred thay are addressed as deans (also, by courtesy, if it is known that they wish to retain the title), except that the envelope would be addressed in the personal name, thus:

> The Very Revd. Charles Cox, D.D.

Provosts

are the incumbents of those parish churches which have become cathedrals in recent times. They take rank and precedence as deans and are addressed in speech as Mr Provost. The most formal manner of address in writing is:

> Very Reverend Sir,
> > I have the honour to remain, Very Reverend Sir,
> > > Your obedient servant,

Less formally, but not socially or on a church matter:

> Dear Sir,
> > Yours faithfully,

The social manner of address in writing is:

> Dear Mr Provost,   *or*
> Dear Provost,
> > Yours sincerely,

Address of envelope in both cases—

> The Very Revd. the Provost of ————.

Retired Provosts

Rules as for retired deans apply.

Archdeacons

are addressed in speech as Mr Archdeacon. The most formal manner of address in writing is:

> Venerable Sir,
> > I have the honour to remain, Venerable Sir,
> > > Your obedient servant,

Less formally, but not socially or on a church matter:

> Dear Sir,
> > Yours faithfully,

The social manner of address in writing is:

> Dear Mr Archdeacon,   *or*
> Dear Archdeacon,
> > Yours sincerely,

> *Address of envelope in both cases—*
> > The Venerable the Archdeacon of ————.

Retired Archdeacons

have no right to the title on retirement, and are addressed as other members of the clergy (*see* p. 128), but if the title Archdeacon Emeritus is conferred on them (also, by courtesy, if it is known that they wish to retain the title), they are addressed in speech as Mr Archdeacon and referred to as Archdeacon ———— (using surname), except in official documents.

> *Address of envelope—*
> > The Venerable Arthur Holt.

Canons

are either residentiary or honorary. The rule is the same in each case. They are addressed in speech as Canon ————. The most formal manner of address in writing is:

> Reverend Sir,
>> I have the honour to remain, Reverend Sir,
>>> Your obedient servant,

Less formally, but not socially or on a church matter:

> Dear Sir,
>> Yours faithfully,

The social manner is:

> Dear Canon,   *or*
> Dear Canon ————,
>> Yours sincerely,

Address of envelope in both cases—

> The Revd. Canon ————.

Minor canons are addressed as other members of the clergy, with no special title.

Prebendaries

are addressed and referred to as Prebendary ————. The most formal manner of address in writing is:

> Reverend Sir,
>> I have the honour to be, Reverend Sir,
>>> Your obedient servant,

Less formally, but not socially or on a church matter:

> Dear Sir,
>> Yours faithfully,

The social manner is:

>   Dear Prebendary, *or*
>   Dear Prebendary ————,
> > Yours sincerely,

Address of envelope in both cases—
> The Revd. Prebendary ————.

Other Members of the Clergy

There is no difference in style of addressing the remaining ranks, although beneficed clergymen are usually called in speech either The Vicar or The Rector. But it is definitely wrong to speak or refer to a clergyman as the Revd. Smith. Initials or name must *always* be used. The style Revd. Mr Smith was common in England within living memory, but its use is now confined to North America, where it is correct. (It may still be used here, if initials or Christian name are not known.) When the name of a clergyman and his wife appear together, the correct form is:

> The Revd. A. B. and Mrs. Smith.

The most formal manner of address in writing is:

>   Reverend Sir, *or*
>   Sir,
> > I beg to remain, Reverend Sir (or Sir),
> > Your obedient servant,

Less formally:

>   Dear Sir,
> > Yours faithfully,

The social manner is:

>   Dear Mr Smith, *or* Dear Rector (or Vicar),
> > Yours sincerely,

Address of envelope in both cases—
> The Revd. A. B. Smith.

Titled Clerics

A temporal title is always preceded in writing by the spiritual one.

> *Examples.*—The Right Revd. and Right Hon. the Lord Bishop of London.
> The Revd. Lord John Smith.
> The Revd. The Hon. David Jones.
> The Revd. Sir John Bull, Bt.

No ordained priest of the Church can receive the accolade of knighthood, but in some cases an appointment to an order of knighthood is made which carries the designation (e.g. K.C.V.O.) without the title. The initials follow the name in the usual way:

> The Right Revd. John Brown, K.C.V.O.,

or, where the see rather than the name is used,

> The Right Revd. the Lord Bishop of ————, K.C.V.O.

The wife of a priest so honoured is not styled or addressed Lady.

Members of Anglican Religious Communities

The head of a community is addressed in writing as The Right Revd. the Lord Abbot, The Revd. (or The Revd. Father) Superior, or The Revd. the Prior, according to his office as head of that community. The initials of the community (should it use them) are added immediately after the name, even if there are decorations or degrees as well. The letter should begin Dear Abbot (or Prior or Superior).

An ordained member of a community is addressed, for example:

The Revd. (or The Revd. Father) A. B. Smith, S.S.J.E.
The Revd. (or The Revd. Father) J. L. Read, C.R., D.D.

A lay member is addressed:

> Brother John, *or*
> Brother John Green.

Benedictines, whether ordained or lay, are addressed as Dom:

> The Revd. Dom James Martin, O.S.B., *or*
> Dom James Martin, O.S.B., if a lay member.

The head of a community for women is addressed as The Revd.
Mother Superior, or The Revd. The Prioress, according to her
office. Ordinary members of the community are addressed by
their Christian, or by their Christian and surnames, according to
the custom of the community, preceded by Sister and followed by
the initials of the community.

Chancellors

are the judges of the Episcopal Courts and the principal lay
officers of the respective dioceses. They are usually, but not
invariably, barristers. The title is used only in connection with
official duties. By the clergy and others within the diocese they
should be called in speech Mr Chancellor, or, more familiarly,
Chancellor. In court, Sir, Worshipful Sir (*not* Your Worship) and
The Learned Chancellor are correct. In writing, Sir, Dear Sir, or,
less formally, Dear Mr Chancellor, should be used.

The envelope should be addressed—

> The Worshipful Chancellor Smith, *or*
> The Worshipful Thomas Smith, *or*
> The Worshipful Sir Thomas Smith (if a knight).

A lady will be addressed as Worshipful Madam, or Madam
Chancellor.

If the chancellor is a Q.C. this should come after the name.

Chancellors of cathedrals are clergymen and should be addressed by clerical title.

The Roman Catholic Church

It should be understood that the following rules have no legal foundation in this country. Roman Catholic archbishops and bishops have no claim to territorial titles or to the use of the salutations Your Grace or My Lord, and such modes of address are not permitted in official documents and circles. But unofficially and within the Roman Catholic community this chapter holds good.

The Pope

is the supreme head on earth of the Roman Catholic Church, and is personally addressed and referred to as Your Holiness or His Holiness.

Style of Addressing in Writing

The formal manner in English is:

Your Holiness,
> I have the honour to remain,
> Your Holiness's most devoted and obedient child,

or

Most Holy Father,
> Your Holiness's most humble child,

A non-Roman Catholic may subscribe himself "servant" and not "child".

Address of envelope—
> His Holiness The Pope.

Letters addressed to the Pope would normally go through

ecclesiastical channels, and if written in English would be translated into Latin.

Cardinals

are addressed and referred to in speech both formally and socially as Your Eminence and His Eminence.

The most formal manner of address in writing is:

> My Lord Cardinal, *or*
> Your Eminence,
>> I have the honour to remain, my Lord Cardinal,
>>> Your Eminence's devoted and obedient child,

Less formally:

> Your Eminence,
>> I remain, Your Eminence,
>>> Yours faithfully,

The social manner in writing is:

> Dear Cardinal ————,
>> Yours sincerely,

Address of envelope in each case—

> His Eminence Cardinal ————.

Cardinal Archbishops

Rules as for CARDINALS apply here, except as to the address of envelope, which should be:

> His Eminence the Cardinal Archbishop of ————.

> *or, preferably,*

> His Eminence Cardinal ————, Archbishop of ————,

since the dignity of Cardinal is personal, and not attached to the office of Archbishop. The same rule should be followed for Cardinals who are Bishops.

Archbishops

are addressed and referred to in speech both formally and socially as Your Grace and His Grace. The most formal manner of address in writing is:

>My Lord Archbishop,   *or*
>Your Grace,
>>I have the honour to remain, my Lord Archbishop,
>>Your Grace's devoted and obedient child,

Less formally:

>Your Grace,
>>Yours faithfully,

The social manner is:

>Dear Archbishop,
>>Yours sincerely,

Address of envelope—

>His Grace The Archbishop of ————,   *or*
>The Most Revd. James Smith, Archbishop of ————.

The Archbishop of Armagh is the Primate of All Ireland, and the Archbishop of Dublin is the Primate of Ireland. In these cases the second form is appropriate:

>>The Most Revd. James Smith,
>>Archbishop of Armagh and Primate
>>of All Ireland;

>>The Most Revd. James Smith,
>>Archbishop of Dublin and Primate
>>of Ireland.

Retired archbishops are addressed by name:
>>The Most Revd. Archbishop Smith.

Form used by officials within the British Commonwealth:

Most Reverend Sir,
>> I (We) have the honour to be,
>>> Your faithful servant(s),

Address of envelope—
>> The Most Revd. Archbishop Brown.

Bishops

The manner of address in speech both formally and socially is My Lord and His Lordship. The most formal manner of address in writing is:

My Lord,   *or*
My Lord Bishop,
>> I have the honour to remain,
>>> Your Lordship's obedient servant (or child),

Less formally:
>> My Lord,

>>> Yours faithfully,

The social manner is:
>> Dear Bishop,

>>> Yours sincerely,

Address of envelope in both cases—

The Right Revd. James Smith, Bishop of ————, *or*
His Lordship the Bishop of ————.

Retired bishops are addressed by name:
>> The Right Revd. Bishop Smith.

Form used by officials within the British Commonwealth:
>> Right Reverend Sir,
>>> I (We) have the honour to be,
>>>> Your faithful servant(s),

Address of envelope—

> The Right Revd. Bishop Brown.

Irish Bishops

The foregoing rules apply, except that the envelope is addressed:

> The Most Revd. the Bishop of —————.

Bishops in other English-speaking countries are customarily also addressed as Most Revd.

Bishops Coadjutor

are appointed to assist a bishop or archbishop, and will normally succeed him on his retirement. They are addressed as bishops, using the personal name:

The Right Revd. William Flynn, Bishop Coadjutor of —————.

Bishops Auxiliary

are also appointed to assist an archbishop or a bishop, but without the expectation of succession. They are addressed in the same way as a bishop coadjutor, adding their office on the envelope:

The Right Revd. John Haines, Bishop Auxiliary of —————.

Titular Sees

Foregoing rules for Archbishops and Bishops apply, except as to envelopes, which are addressed:

> The Most Revd. Archbishop Brown.
> The Right Revd. (or Most Revd.) Bishop Brown.

It is unnecessary to refer to the titular see.

Provosts

are addressed in speech as Provost ————. The most formal manner of address in writing is:

> Very Reverend Sir,
>> I have the honour to remain, Very Reverend Sir,
>> Your obedient servant,

Less formally:
> Dear Sir,
>> Yours faithfully,

The social manner of address in writing is:

> Dear Provost ————, *or*
> Dear Provost,
>> Yours sincerely,

Address of envelope—
> The Very Revd. Provost ————.

Canons

Canons are addressed and referred to in speech as Canon ————. The most formal manner of address in writing is:

> Very Reverend Sir,
>> I have the honour to remain, Very Reverend Sir,
>> Your obedient servant,

Less formally:
> Dear Sir,
>> Yours faithfully,

The social manner of address in writing is:

> Dear Canon ————, *or*
> Dear Canon,
>> Yours sincerely,

Address of envelope—

> The Very Revd. Canon ————.

If he is a Monsignore, this is added: The Very Revd. Monsignor (Canon) ————. Both titles may be used, but it is unnecessary.

Monsignori

are addressed and referred to in speech, both formally and socially, as Monsignor Smith, or as Monsignore. They may be Protonotaries, Domestic Prelates, Privy Chamberlains, or Honorary Chamberlains of His Holiness the Pope. The most formal manner of address is:

> Reverend Sir,
>> I have the honour to remain, Reverend Sir,
>>> Your devoted and obedient servant,

Less formally:

> Reverend Sir,
>> Yours faithfully,

The social manner of address is:

> Dear Monsignore,   *or*
> Dear Monsignor Smith,
>> Yours sincerely,

Address of envelope—

> The Revd. Mgr. Vincent Smith,   *or*
> The Revd. Monsignore.

Abbots

Abbots are addressed and referred to in speech as Father Abbot. The most formal manner of address in writing is:

My Lord Abbot,   *or*
Right Reverend Abbot ————,   *or*
Right Reverend Father,
> I beg to remain, my Lord Abbot (or alternatives),
> > Your devoted and obedient servant,

Less formally:

My Lord Abbot,
> Yours faithfully,

The social manner of address is:

Dear Father Abbot,
> Yours sincerely,

Address of envelope—

The Right Revd. the Abbot of Thornton (with distinguishing initials of his order).

Benedictine Abbots do not use the designation "Lord Abbot".

Provincials

are addressed and referred to in speech as Father ————.
The most formal manner of address in writing is:

Very Reverend Father,
> I beg to remain, Very Reverend Father,
> > Your devoted and obedient child,

Less formally:

Very Reverend Father,
> Yours faithfully,

The social manner of address is:

Dear Father ————, *or*
Dear Father Provincial,
> Yours sincerely,

Address of envelope—
> The Very Revd. Father ————,   *or*
> The Very Revd. Father Provincial (with distinguishing initials of his order).

Benedictines

are called Dom. The formal manner of address in writing is:

> Dear Reverend Father,

while the social manner of address is:

> Dear Dom Henry Smith,   *or*
> Dear Dom Henry,

Address of envelope—
> The Revd. Dom H. Smith, O.S.B.

Priests

are addressed and referred to in speech as Father ————.

The most formal manner of address in writing is:

> Dear Reverend Father,
>> Your devoted and obedient child,

Less formally:

> Dear Reverend Father,
>> Yours faithfully,

The social manner of address in writing is:

> Dear Father ————,
>> Yours sincerely,

Address of envelope—
> The Revd. Father ————.

Titled Priests

As with the clergy of the Church of England (*see* p. 129), the spiritual title always precedes the temporal one.

Roman Catholic clergy do, however, use the title Sir if they become a member of an order of knighthood; the former Archbishop of Sydney, for example, was known as His Eminence Sir Norman Cardinal Gilroy, KBE.

Women in Religious Communities

The head of a community may be called Abbess, Prioress, Superior, or Reverend Mother. She will be addressed according to her office, with the addition of the letters of her order:

The Lady Abbess,
The Reverend Mother Prioress,
The Reverend Mother,
The Mother Superior,
The Sister Superior.

Letters should begin:

Dear Lady Abbess,
Dear Reverend Mother,
Dear Sister Superior.

Other members of the order are addressed as The Reverend Sister, with Christian name, or Christian and surname, according to the custom of the order, and with the letters of the order, if used.

The Church of Scotland

The Lord High Commissioner to the General Assembly

is addressed and referred to as Your Grace and His Grace during his term of office. The formal manner of address in writing is:

Your Grace,
> I have the honour to remain,
> Your Grace's most devoted and obedient servant,

Address of envelope—
> His Grace the Lord High Commissioner.

The social manner of address is the same, viz. Your Grace, etc., except when the office is held by a member of the Royal Family, in which case the formal and social address may be either Your Royal Highness or Your Grace.

The Moderator

is addressed in speech as Moderator, or as Dr ————— (or Mr —————, as the case may be). The most formal manner of address in writing is:

Right Reverend Sir,
> I beg to remain, Right Reverend Sir,
> Your obedient servant,

Less formally:

Dear Sir,   *or*
Dear Moderator,
> Yours faithfully,

The social manner of address in writing is:

Dear Moderator,   *or*
Dear Dr (or Mr) Smith,
> Yours sincerely,

Address of envelope—
> The Right Revd. the Moderator of the General Assembly of the Church of Scotland.

Ex-Moderators

These dignitaries are designated The Very Reverend.
The most formal manner of address in writing is:

> Very Reverend Sir,
> > I beg to remain, Very Reverend Sir,
> > > Your obedient servant,

Less formally:

> Dear Sir,   *or*
> Dear Minister,
> > Yours faithfully,

The social manner of address in writing is-

> Dear Dr (or Mr) Smith,
> > Yours sincerely,

> *Address of envelope in both cases—*
> The Very Revd. Albert Smith (and if a Dr), D.D.

Dean of the Thistle and Chapel Royal

Rules as for DEANS of the Church of England apply here (*see* p. 124).

Other Members of the Clergy

Rules as for the Church of England apply (*see* p. 128), except that the titles of Vicar and Rector are not used. A minister in a regular parochial charge is often called The Minister (of the parish) or the Parish Minister, and envelopes are addressed The Minister of ―――.

Other Free Churches

Ministers of the Free Churches are addressed formally:

Dear Sir,   *or*
Dear Minister,
                    Yours faithfully,
(For women Ministers, Dear Madam).

The social manner of address in writing is:

Dear Mr (or Dr) Smith,
                    Yours sincerely,

Address of envelope—

The Revd. Matthew Smith,   *or*
The Revd. Margaret Smith.

"The Revd. Smith" is in all cases incorrect, and "Revd. Smith"
even more so.

The Eastern Church

Patriarchs

are personally addressed and referred to as Your Holiness or His
Holiness. The style of address in writing is:

Your Holiness,
            I have the honour to be, Sir,
                    Your Holiness's obedient servant,

Address of envelope—

His Holiness The Patriarch.

Metropolitans

are personally addressed and referred to as Your Grace and His
Grace. The style of address in writing is:

Your Grace,
            I am, Sir,
                    Your Grace's obedient servant,

Address of envelope—

> His Beatitude The Metropolitan of ————.

Archbishops and Bishops

as for Anglican Archbishops and Bishops (*see* pp. 118 and 121).

Archimandrites

Archimandrites are addressed and referred to in speech as Right Reverend Father. The formal manner of address in writing is:

> Right Reverend Father,
>> I beg to remain, Right Reverend Father,
>>> Your obedient servant,

The social manner is:

> Dear Father,
>> Yours sincerely,

Other Denominations

As a matter of courtesy, rules as for OTHER CLERGY of the Church of England apply (*see* p. 128).

The Jewish Synagogue

Ministers

are addressed and referred to in speech as Mr Cohen or Dr Cohen, according to degree. The most formal manner of address in writing is:

> Reverend and dear Sir,
>> I am, Reverend Sir,
>>> Your obedient servant,

Less formally:

>Dear Sir,
>
>>Yours faithfully,

The social manner of address is:

>Dear Mr (or Dr) Cohen,
>>Yours sincerely,

Address of envelope in each case—

>>The Revd. A. Cohen,   *or*
>>The Revd. Dr A. Cohen.

Rabbis

are addressed and referred to in speech as Rabbi Cohen. The most formal manner of address in writing is:

>Reverend and dear Sir,
>>I am, Reverend Sir,
>>>Your obedient servant,

Less formally:

>Dear Sir,
>
>>Yours faithfully,

The social manner of address is:

>Dear Rabbi Cohen,
>>Yours sincerely,

Address of envelope—

>>The Revd. Rabbi A. Cohen.

Rabbi Doctors

are addressed and referred to in speech as Dr Cohen. The social manner of address is:

>Dear Dr Cohen,
>>Yours sincerely,

Address of envelope—

> The Revd. Rabbi Dr A. Cohen.

The Chief Rabbi

is addressed and referred to in speech as Chief Rabbi. The most formal manner of address in writing is:

> Very Reverend and dear Sir,
>> I am, Very Reverend Sir,
>>> Your obedient servant,

Less formally:

> Dear Sir,

>> Yours faithfully,

The social manner of address in writing is:

> Dear Chief Rabbi,

>> Yours sincerely,

Address of envelope—

>> The Very Revd. the Chief Rabbi,   *or*
>> The Chief Rabbi Dr J. Cohen.

THE ROYAL NAVY

This is the senior fighting service. Titles which have duplicates in the Army rank higher in the Navy. In these cases, and indeed for all ranks below Rear-Admiral, the words Royal Navy, or more usually in ordinary correspondence the abbreviation R.N. will be added after the name, and any decorations and orders. All ranks above that of sub-lieutenant are addressed and referred to in speech by their service title (unless they possess a higher title otherwise). Decorations and honours should never be omitted from envelopes. A few general rules are given below.

Admirals of the Fleet

Address of envelopes both formally and socially:
    Admiral of the Fleet Lord (or any other title) ————.

In other respects according to peerage or other rank.

Admirals

Vice-Admirals

Rear-Admirals

All are addressed in speech as Admiral ————. Only on envelopes are the graded titles used.

The most formal manner of address in writing is:

Sir,

I have the honour to remain, Sir,
Your obedient servant,

Less formally:

>Dear Sir,

>>Yours faithfully,

The social manner is by his title if he has one, otherwise:

>Dear Admiral Flint,

although officers of this rank may express a preference for being addressed by rank rather than by title; if so their preference should be followed.

Commodores

The rank is held by senior captains in special appointments. The title is used in speech both formally and socially. The most formal manner is:

>Sir,

>>I have the honour to be, Sir,
>>>Your obedient servant,

Less formally:

>Dear Sir,

>>Yours faithfully,

The social manner is:

>Dear Commodore Beal,

>>Yours sincerely,

>*Address of envelope in every case—*

>>Commodore A. Beal, Royal Navy.

Captains

The title is used in speech both formally and socially. The most formal manner of address in writing is:

Sir,

I have the honour to be, Sir,
Your obedient servant,

Less formally:

Dear Sir,

Yours faithfully,

The social manner of address in writing is:

Dear Captain Birch,

Yours sincerely,

Address of envelope in both cases—

Captain A. B. Birch, Royal Navy.

Commanders

This title is used both formally and socially in speech.

Address of envelope in both cases—

Commander C. D. Bartlett, Royal Navy.

Lieutenant-Commanders

are addressed in speech as Commander. Only on envelopes is the graded title used.

Lieutenants

are addressed officially in speech as Lieutenant and socially as Mr.

Address of envelope in either case—

Lieutenant G. H. Crane, Royal Navy.

Sub-Lieutenants

Midshipmen

Cadets

All are addressed in social and official speech as Mr. Official and social envelopes are addressed:

> Sub.-Lieut. I. J. Drake, Royal Navy.
> Midshipman K. L. Blake, Royal Navy.
> Cadet M. N. Hawke, Royal Navy.

Retired Officers

A retired officer should be addressed in exactly the same way as one on the active list, except that the abbreviation 'Rtd' should be added whenever it is necessary to indicate the fact. For instance, a private letter should be addressed without the suffix, but a letter to a retired officer working, say in the Ministry of Defence, or for a ship-builder, should add 'Rtd'.

Titled Officers

A hereditary or conferred title is preceded by the naval one.

> *Examples.*—Admiral Sir Norman Blake.
>   Captain the Hon. Norman Birch, Royal Navy.

Chaplains

The Chaplain of the Fleet is an Archdeacon, and is addressed accordingly. The envelope may be addressed to The Chaplain of the Fleet, or with this designation added to the name. Other chaplains are addressed as clergymen with the words Royal Navy attached to their name.

Decorations

Abbreviations are used immediately after the name thus:

> Captain O. P. Hawke, D.S.O., Royal Navy.
> Lieut. A. R. Crane, D.S.C., Royal Navy.

They should, of course, never be omitted.

General List and Medical Officers

The foregoing rules apply to all officers on the General List (i.e. Seaman, Engineering, Electrical Engineering, and Supply & Secretariat specialists). Similar rules apply to Medical Officers, except that their ranks should, in speech and writing, be prefixed by the name of their branch:

> Surgeon-Commander S. T. Brice.

Royal Marines

Officers of the Royal Marines have Army ranks, and are addressed in the same way, with the letters R.M. following the name if their rank is Lieutenant-Colonel or below. (*See* p. 157.)

THE ARMY

All ranks above that of lieutenant are addressed and referred to in speech by their service title (unless they possess a higher one otherwise). Decorations and honours should never be omitted from envelopes.

Field-Marshals

Address of envelope, both formally and socially:

> Field-Marshal Lord (or any other title) ————.

In other respects according to peerage or other rank.

Generals

Lieutenant-Generals

Major-Generals

All are addressed in speech as General ————. Only on envelopes are the graded titles used. The formal manner of address in writing is Sir, the social manner is Dear General Sands, or by his title if he has one, according to his preference.

Brigadiers

Addressed in speech and on envelopes as Brigadier Blank. The formal manner of address in writing is Sir, the social manner is Dear Brigadier Blank.

Colonels

Addressed in speech and on envelopes as Colonel Howe. The

formal manner of address in writing is Sir, and the social manner Dear Colonel Howe.

Lieutenant-Colonels

are addressed in speech as Colonel. Only on envelopes is the graded title used. The regiment is added after the name, and any distinctions he may possess, thus:

> Lieut.-Colonel H. Newcombe, D.S.O., R.H.A.

The formal manner of address in writing is Sir, the social manner Dear Colonel Newcombe.

Majors

Captains

Addressed in speech as Major Shaw and Captain Shaw respectively. The formal manner of address in writing is Sir, the social manner Dear Major (or Captain) Shaw.

Address of envelope—

> Major (or Captain) E. Shaw, 11th Hussars.

Lieutenants

Second-Lieutenants

Addressed in speech as Mr. The formal manner in writing is Sir, the social manner Dear Mr Fry.

Address of official and service envelopes—

> Lieut. (or 2nd Lieut.) T. W. Fry, 2nd Life Guards.

Address of social envelope—

> T. W. Fry, Esq., 2nd Life Guards.

Retired Officers

do not have a regiment appended to their names. It used to be the practice for retired officers under the rank of Major to drop their title, but now a retired captain will be addressed by his rank if he chooses to use it.

Chaplains

The Chaplain-General to the Forces ranks as major-general, and there are four classes below him, ranking respectively as colonels, lieut.-colonels, majors, and captains, but they are addressed in speech and in writing according to their rank as clergymen. The Chaplain-General himself is an Archdeacon. Envelopes to the chaplain-general are addressed To The Chaplain-General of the Forces, and other chaplains have the abbreviation C.F. or S.C.F. added to the name. In no circumstances should military titles be used.

Titled Officers

A hereditary or conferred title is preceded by the military one, as

> Colonel Lord John Bull, 10th Lancers.
> General Sir James Horn.

Decorations

Abbreviations are shown immediately after the name, thus:

> Colonel Newcombe, V.C.
> T. W. Fry, Esq., M.C., 2nd Life Guards.

They should, of course, never be omitted.

THE ROYAL AIR FORCE

The rules relating to the Navy and the Army apply in general. All service titles are used officially, but service titles below that of Flight Lieutenant are not used socially. Decorations and honours should never be omitted from envelopes, and are placed immediately after the name. The abbreviation R.A.F. is placed after decorations and honours below the rank of Air Commodore.

Marshals of the Royal Air Force

Address all envelopes, both formally and socially:

Marshal of the Royal Air Force Lord (or any other title) ————.

In other respects according to peerage or other title.

Air Chief Marshals
Air Marshals
Air Vice-Marshals

Addressed in speech as Air Marshal, but the professional title is never further abbreviated. Only on envelopes are graded professional titles used. The formal manner of address in writing is Sir, the social manner in writing is Dear Air Marshal (or Air Marshal Smith), or by his title if he has one, according to his preference.

Air Commodores

Addressed formally in speech and in writing as Air Commodore Jones. Socially addressed in speech as Air Commodore Jones. The professional title is never abbreviated in social usage. Air Commodores and above are officially graded as "air officers".

Group Captains
Wing Commanders
Squadron Leaders

These senior officer grades are addressed by their service titles, which—in the social manner—are never abbreviated. May be spoken of as the Group Captain, or Group Captain White, or directly addressed Squadron Leader or Squadron Leader Black.

Flight Lieutenants

Addressed by service title which—in the social manner—is never abbreviated. Spoken of as Flight Lieutenant Brown, but not as Flight Lieutenant.

Flying Officers
Pilot Officers

The service titles are used only for official purposes. Social manner of address is Mr Gray. Envelopes should be addressed:

A. B. Gray Esq., D.F.C. (or other decorations if any), R.A.F.

Chaplains

The Chaplain-in-Chief, Royal Air Force has the relative rank of Air Vice-Marshal, and other Royal Air Force Chaplains have ranks relative to Group Captain down to Flight Lieutenant.

Chaplains are, however, known and addressed both officially and otherwise according to their ecclesiastical titles, which for the Chaplain-in-Chief is Archdeacon, and not by their relative status in the Royal Air Force. For example, an envelope should be addressed:

The Reverend A. Green, R.A.F.
and not as Squadron Leader the Rev. A. Green.

COMPARATIVE RANKS IN H.M. FIGHTING FORCES

ROYAL NAVY	ARMY	ROYAL AIR FORCE
ADMIRAL OF THE FLEET	FIELD-MARSHAL	MARSHAL OF THE ROYAL AIR FORCE
ADMIRAL	GENERAL	AIR CHIEF MARSHAL
VICE-ADMIRAL	LIEUTENANT-GENERAL	AIR MARSHAL
REAR-ADMIRAL	MAJOR-GENERAL	AIR VICE-MARSHAL
COMMODORE	BRIGADIER	AIR COMMODORE
CAPTAIN	COLONEL	GROUP CAPTAIN
COMMANDER	LIEUTENANT-COLONEL	WING COMMANDER
LIEUTENANT-COMMANDER	MAJOR	SQUADRON LEADER
LIEUTENANT	CAPTAIN	FLIGHT LIEUTENANT
SUB-LIEUTENANT	LIEUTENANT	FLYING OFFICER
	SECOND LIEUTENANT	PILOT OFFICER

In the Royal Marines ranks compare with Navy ranks as Army ranks do down to Colonel; but Colonel and Lieutenant-Colonel R.M. are both the equivalent of a Captain R.N., and a Major R.M. of a Commander R.N., and so on down.

THE WOMEN'S SERVICES

The comparative ranks in the Women's Services are given in the table below. Their use is, in general, the same as for Military, Naval and Air Force ranks, except that Madam is used instead of Sir (Ma'am would ordinarily be used in speaking).

W.R.A.C.	W.R.N.S.	W.R.A.F.
Major-General	Chief Commandant	Air Marshal
Brigadier	Commandant	Air Commodore
Colonel	Superintendent	Group Captain
Lieut.-Colonel	Chief Officer	Wing Commander
Major	First Officer	Squadron Leader
Captain	Second Officer	Flight Lieutenant
Lieutenant	Third Officer	Flying Officer
2nd Lieutenant	—	Pilot Officer

LAW, DIPLOMATIC AND GOVERNMENT

The various titles and offices are given alphabetically.

Agents-General

These are the representatives in London of the provincial or state governments (not the Federal Governments) of Canada or Australia. They are addressed according to their own name and rank, with their office following the name on an envelope.

Aldermen

(This paragraph now applies only to Aldermen of the Corporation of London and in certain parts of Northern Ireland, since the office has been abolished elsewhere.)

Addressed during office as Alderman. Official letters begin:

Dear Sir,

Social letters begin:

Dear Alderman, *or* Dear Alderman Jones.

Address of envelope—

Mr Alderman J. Jones.

If an Alderman possesses another title this should of course be used; in such cases Alderman precedes other designations; Mr, Mrs or Miss, however, are used before the word Alderman.

Alderman Sir Joseph Jones.
Mrs Alderman Jones.

Ambassadors

The formal and social manner of address in speech is Your Excellency or Sir. The formal manner of address in writing is:

> My Lord (or Sir, according to rank),
> > I have the honour to be, my Lord (or Sir),
> > > Your Excellency's obedient servant,

The social manner in writing is:

> Dear Mr Whitby (Sir Charles, or according to rank),
> > Yours sincerely.

Address of envelope (formal or social)—

> > His Excellency Mr Charles Whitby, C.M.G. (not Esq.)
> > > (Sir Charles Whitby, K.C.M.G.),
> > > > H.M. Embassy,

American ambassadors: The Honorable Charles Whitby

Ambassadors' wives do not share their husbands' official title of Excellency, although it is still accorded them by courtesy in some countries, and the usage has not entirely ceased in others.

Attorneys-General

are addressed in speech according to their own name and rank. They are invariably Q.C.s and rules as for Queen's Counsel apply. On envelopes they may be addressed as The Attorney-General or by their name and rank.

Bailies (of Scottish Burghs)

Addressed during office as Bailie. Social letters begin:

> Dear Bailie Campbell,

Address of envelope—

> > Bailie J. Campbell.

Chairman of the Greater London Council

Rules as for privy counsellors apply (*see* p. 116), except that the prefix Right Hon. ceases on retirement.

Address of envelope—

The Right Hon. the Chairman of the Greater London Council,

or

The Right Hon. James Brown, but, on retirement,
James Brown, Esq.

Chairmen of County Councils

The Chairman of a County Council is addressed as Mr Chairman, even though the Chairman for the time being be a lady. Official envelopes are addressed

The Chairman of ———— County Council,

except that the Chairman of the Greater London Council is addressed as The Right Honourable (*see* above).

Chairmen of District Councils

Since local government reorganisation cities and towns which once called their civic heads Lord Mayor or Mayor, Lord Provost or Provost in Scotland, have become districts, and their civic heads Chairmen of District Councils. Nevertheless, in those cities and towns which had Mayors or Provosts in the past the Chairman of the District Council may still be so described, and the forms of address shown under Lord Mayor, Lord Provost, Mayor and Provost still apply (*see* pp. 170, 171, 173, 175). Otherwise they are addressed in the same way as Chairmen of County Councils.

Chargés d'affaires

usually take the place temporarily of ambassadors at embassies and of ministers at legations, while at a few posts the office is a permanent one. They rank below envoys-extraordinary in diplomatic circles, but the same rules apply.

Consuls

Envelopes are addressed—

> To George Smith, Esq.,
> H.M. Agent and Consul-General, *or*
> H.M. Consul-General, *or*
> H.M. Consul, *or*
> H.M. Vice-Consul,

In all other respects as an Esquire (*see* p. 111).

Conveners

The Chairman of a Regional or District Council in Scotland is often known as the Convener or Convenor (both spellings are used). He is addressed in the same way as if he were called Chairman, except that in speech he (or she) is called Convener, without the "Mr".

Councillors

Addressed during office as Councillor. Official letters begin:

> Dear Sir,

Social letters begin:

> Dear Councillor, *or* Dear Councillor Peters.

Address of envelope—

> Councillor S. Peters.

If a Councillor possesses another title this should be used; in such cases Councillor precedes other designations, including Mrs or Miss.

> Councillor Sir Stanley Peters.
> Councillor Mrs Peters.

Mr and Esq. are not used.

It is better not to add the title Councillor to other titles unless writing on Council business.

Deputy Lieutenants of Counties

are addressed in speech according to their own name and rank. For official letters the affix D.L. should be used (*see* pp. 180–181).

Envoys-Extraordinary and Ministers-Plenipotentiary

See under Ministers (Diplomatic Service), p. 174.

Governors-General

Governors

Lieutenant-Governors

Governors-General and Governors are called "His Excellency" while holding office and in their territories; the wives of Governors-General are also so addressed, but not the wives of Governors. The Lieutenant-Governors of Jersey, Guernsey and the Isle of Man have the same style; the Governor-General of Canada is called "Right Honourable" for life, and the Lieutenant-Governors of Canadian provinces are called "The Honourable" for life. (In these cases the title Lieutenant-Governor is given to the person holding the principal office; the deputy of the Governor of an Australian state is also known as Lieutenant-Governor, and he, of course, is not called "His Excellency", or "The Honourable").

Envelopes are addressed—

His Excellency Sir John ————, Governor-General of ————,

His Excellency Mr J. H. ————, Governor and Commander-in-Chief of ————.

H.M. Lord-Lieutenants of Counties.
(*See* Lord-Lieutenants of Counties)

High Commissioners

represent one country of the Commonwealth in another. They are in effect Ambassadors, and are addressed similarly.

Forms of address are as follows:

Formally:

Your Excellency,
            I have the honour to be,
                        Your Excellency's obedient servant,

His Excellency Mr
            The Honourable
            The Right Honourable
            (according to rank)

Socially:

Dear High Commissioner,
            Believe me,
                        Dear High Commissioner,
                        Yours sincerely,
His Excellency Mr ———— (*as above*).

High Sheriffs.
(*See* Sheriffs)

Honourable

The title "The Honourable" is accorded in the Commonwealth and other English-speaking countries to holders of a number of public offices, including Ministers (or their equivalent), Judges, members of *some* legislative bodies, Governors or Lieutenant-Governors, and so on. It may be held for life or during tenure of office; within the scope of this book it is sufficient to say that the usage exists and should be followed where it appears; and that it is not usual to abbreviate "The Honorable" in the United States.

Judges of the High Court

are usually knighted on appointment. They are addressed and referred to as My Lord and Your (or His) Lordship on the Bench, in the precincts of the Court, and whenever they are being approached in their judicial capacity. The formal manner of address in writing is, according to circumstances, either My Lord or Sir.

The address of the envelope is—

The Hon. Mr Justice Swift.

Queen's Counsel who are appointed High Court Judges no longer use the initials after their name.

In their private capacities they may be addressed in speech as "Mr Justice Smith", as "Judge", or as "Sir John", and in writing as:

The Hon. Mr Justice Swift (to a court address), *or*
The Hon. Sir John Swift (to a private address).

As with Circuit Judges (*see* p. 167), the second to be appointed of two High Court Judges with the same name will have chosen to be known by a forename in addition.

The High Court has three divisions, Chancery, Queen's Bench, and Family Divisions, and each division has a President.

The Lord High Chancellor of Great Britain is by virtue of his office President of the Chancery Division, and judge who normally acts for him in that capacity is known as the Vice-Chancellor; the Lord Chief Justice of England is President of the Queen's Bench Divison; and one of the judges of the Family Division is appointed its President. These judges are not addressed as Hon. Mr Justice; the Lord Chancellor and Lord Chief Justice are addressed as such (*see* pp. 169 and 170), and the other two by their names and offices, or by their offices alone:

> The Hon. Sir Charles Brown,
> The Vice-Chancellor,   *or,*
>
> The Vice-Chancellor,
>
> and The Right Hon. Sir Maurice Smith,
> President of the Family Division,   *or,*
>
> The President of the Family Division,

(Hon. or Right Hon. depending on whether the judge is a Privy Counsellor).

In 1965 the first woman Judge of the High Court was appointed, and there are now a number. They are made Dame of the Most Excellent Order of the British Empire on their appointment, and are addressed in Court as My Lady and Your (or Her) Ladyship.

The formal manner of address in writing is:

> The Hon. Mrs Justice ————.

Socially they may be addressed in speech as "Mrs Justice ————" or as "Dame ———— ————". In writing they are addressed as:

> The Hon. Dame ———— ————, D.B.E., *or*
> The Hon. Mrs Justice ————, D.B.E.

The style "Mrs Justice" is used by unmarried judges also.

The prefix "The Honourable" and the style The Hon. Mr Justice are not retained after retirement.

Circuit Judges

Circuit Judges are addressed and referred to on the Bench as Your Honour and His Honour. Socially they are addressed and referred to in conversation as Judge or Judge Jones. Letters are addressed:

Dear Judge, *or* Dear Judge Jones.

Address of envelope both socially and officially—

His Honour Judge Jones.

Queen's Counsel who are appointed Circuit Judges continue to use the initials Q.C. after their names.

Where two judges have the same (or even a very similar) surname, the second to be appointed will choose to be known by one of his forenames as well as his surname; for example, Mr Henry Roberts Jones is made a Circuit Judge, and (because there is already a Judge, or a Mr Justice Jones) is known as His Honour Judge Roberts Jones.

The title His Honour is now retained after retirement, omitting the word Judge, and adding the forename or initials; so that the address of the envelope is:

His Honour Henry Jones.

Judges overseas

Judges of the High Courts or Supreme Courts of Commonwealth countries or overseas territories are addressed during office as:

The Honourable the Chief Justice, *or*
The Hon. Mr Justice ————.

The Chief Justice of Canada bears the title "Right Honour-

able" for life, and other judges of Commonwealth countries may
be Privy Counsellors, when they will be addressed as Right Hon.
also. It is not unusual in some countries for a Judge who has held
office for some time to be granted the title "The Honourable" for
life. Otherwise no special form of address is used on retirement.

Justices of the Peace

Addressed on the Bench as Your Worship, and by letter socially
as an Esquire (*see* p. 111), or according to rank. When writing to a
Justice of the Peace in his official capacity (but only then), the
affix J.P. should be used (*see* pp. 180–181).

Lady Mayoresses

Rules as for wives of Lord Mayors apply (*see* p. 170).

Law Lords.
(*See* LIFE PEERS, p. 43.)

Lord-Lieutenants and Lieutenants of Counties

are addressed according to their rank, e.g.

> His Grace the Duke of Middlesex, K.G.,
> H.M. Lord-Lieutenant for ————.

If he is a commoner the form is:

> A. Smith, Esq.,
> H.M. Lord-Lieutenant for ————.

At the time of the amalgamation of some counties under the
Local Government Act 1972, the appointment formerly known as
H.M. Lieutenant (commonly called Lord Lieutenant), became
officially H.M. Lord-Lieutenant; and some additional appointments were made, so that a new county consisting of two or more

formerly separate counties might have a Lord-Lieutenant and one or two Lieutenants. The appointment of a Lieutenant was only made when the new county included two counties each of which had previously had its own Lord Lieutenant. A Lieutenant is also addressed according to his rank, with the addition of his appointment:

> Colonel J. S. Napier, D.S.O.,
> H.M. Lieutenant for ————.

Lord Advocate of Scotland

Formerly always My Lord, etc.; but latterly, probably from ceasing to be on the Bench, frequently as Sir; but is socially addressed as Lord Advocate, and in writing Dear Lord Advocate. He may be a member of the House of Lords or of the House of Commons, but need not be either; he is always a Privy Counsellor.

Envelopes are addressed—

> The Right Hon. the Lord Advocate.

Lord of Appeal in Ordinary

and his wife and children. Rules as for BARONS and BARONESSES apply (*see* pp. 84 to 90).

Lord Chamberlain

is addressed according to rank and title.

Lord Chancellor

The Lord Chancellor is addressed as Lord Chancellor, and referred to in speech and writing either by his appointment or according to his rank in the peerage. Envelopes are addressed both formally and socially:

The Right Hon. the Lord Chancellor *or*

in the most formal circumstances:

The Right Hon. the Lord High Chancellor of Great Britain.

Lord Chief Justice

He is a peer, and is addressed and referred to accordingly; alternatively a social letter may begin:

Dear Lord Chief Justice

Envelopes are addressed both formally and socially—

The Right Hon. the Lord Chief Justice of England.

Lord Justice of Appeal

Addressed and referred to as My Lord and His Lordship and by professional and semi-professional or semi-official correspondents as

Dear Lord Justice.

Envelopes are addressed—

The Right Hon. the Lord Justice ————;

Privately, they may be addressed—

The Right Hon. Sir Henry ————.

In speech, he may be called socially Sir Henry.

Lord Mayors

The Lord Mayors of Belfast, Cardiff, Dublin, London, and York, and of the Australian cities of Adelaide, Brisbane, Hobart, Melbourne, Sydney, and Perth are entitled to the style Right Hon. while they are in office. This is, however, only an official and not a personal prefix, and it is used only with the title "Lord

Mayor" and not with the Lord Mayor's own name; it is incorrect
to address such a Lord Mayor as, for example, "The Right Hon.
Richard Whittington". Their wives (or the lady acting as Lady
Mayoress) do not share the honour of the style Right Hon.

The formal mode of address both in speech and writing is My
Lord and My Lady, while socially they are addressed according
to their own name and rank except on the envelope.

Address of envelope, formally and socially—

> The Right Hon. the Lord Mayor of ————.
> The Lady Mayoress of ————.

The Mayors of certain other cities also are designated "Lord
Mayors", and are addressed according to these rules, except as to
envelope, which should be addressed

> The Right Worshipful the Lord Mayor of ————.
> The Lady Mayoress of ————.

The form of address does not vary when the Lord Mayor is a
lady.

Lord Privy Seal

is addressed according to his own name and title.

Lord Provosts

Under the Local Government (Scotland) Act, 1973, the title of
Lord Provost attaches to the Chairmen of the District Councils of
Dundee, Aberdeen, Edinburgh and Glasgow. During office they
are addressed and referred to as My Lord and His Lordship.

Envelopes are addressed—

> The Lord Provost of ————.

but the Lord Provost of Edinburgh is entitled to the words "The
Right Hon." in front of his name, and the Lord Provost of

Glasgow is known as "The Right Hon. the Lord Provost of Glasgow" and socially referred to as The Lord Provost; in social address Lord Provost, not (except in historical comparison) "Lord Provost Campbell", and addressed as The Lord Provost of —————. Letters begin

> Dear Lord Provost.

Their wives do not share the title, though there is a recent tendency to refer to them as The Lady Provost, which has led to such incorrect descriptions as "Lord Provost Campbell and the Lady Provost of —————", which should be avoided.

Lord of Session

is a Judge of the Court of Session (or Senator of the College of Justice), of Scotland, who upon elevation to the Bench is styled for life The Hon. Lord, with his surname or a territorial name according to his choice. This is a title of judicial office, and not a peerage.

Envelopes are addressed—

> The Hon. Lord —————.

His wife is addressed in writing as Lady —————, and in other respects as the wife of a Baron (*see* p. 84), but without the prefix "The Right Hon.", or "The". Their children have no title. If a Lord of Session is also a Privy Counsellor he is of course addressed as The Right Hon. Lord —————. The Lord Justice-General and the Lord Justice-Clerk of Scotland are Lords of Session; they are Privy Counsellors, and are always addressed by their office:

> The Right Hon. the Lord Justice-General,
> The Right Hon. the Lord Justice-Clerk.

Upon giving up this office they revert to the style of a Lord of Session who is a Privy Counsellor.

Magistrates

See under Justices of the Peace (p. 168), and Stipendiary Magistrates (p. 177).

Master of the Rolls

Rules as for JUDGES apply (*see* p. 165).

Address of envelope—

>   The Right Hon. The Master of the Rolls,   *or*
>   The Right Hon. (according to rank).

Masters of the Supreme Court

are addressed according to own name and rank, except in court, when they are addressed and referred to as Master Robson.

Mayors when Ladies

are addressed as "Your Worship" or "Mr Mayor"; colloquially "Madam Mayor" is sometimes used, but this is not an established mode of address.

Mayoresses

are addressed as "Mayoress", never "Your Worship", or "Mr Mayor", but if a Mayoress is a J.P. and is sitting on the Bench, the term "Your Worship" would of course be used when addressing the Bench.

Mayors

Addressed as an Esquire (*see* p. 111), or according to own rank.

Envelopes are addressed—

>   If mayor of a city:
>   The Right Worshipful the Mayor of ————.

If mayor of a borough:
The Worshipful the Mayor of ————.

The Mayors of certain cities use the description "Lord Mayor" (*see* p. 170 under that heading).

Members of Parliament

According to rank, with M.P. after the name.

Ministers (Diplomatic Service)

The title Envoy-Extraordinary and Minister-Plenipotentiary, given to the head of a Legation, was cutomarily abbreviated to Minister. Now all posts have been elevated to Ambassador, and all Legations to Embassy, with one exception: the British representative at the Holy See is still styled Minister. He is addressed as His Excellency, and in all ways as though he were an Ambassador, except for the title itself.

Ministers, Ministers (Economic), or Ministers (Commercial) may serve under the Ambassador in a large Embassy; but their title merely indicates their diplomatic service rank and they are not given any special form of address, as they would be if they were Ministers Plenipotentiary at the head of a Legation.

Police

Policemen or women of the rank of Commissioner, or Deputy or Assistant Commissioner (in the Metropolitan and City of London Police), and Chief Constable, or Deputy or Assistant Chief Constable (in other Police Forces), are addressed in speech, and socially in writing, either by name or by appointment; formal letters begin

Dear Sir,

social ones either

Dear Mr Dixon,   *or*
Dear Chief Constable;

the envelope is addressed with the name, followed by appointment and Force:

Sir George Dixon, C.B.E.,
Commissioner of Police of the
Metropolis;

George Dixon Esq., O.B.E.,
Deputy Chief Constable, ————
Constabulary.

Commanders, Chief Superintendents and Superintendents may be addressed either with the rank before the name or as Mr (Mrs, or Miss) Dixon; envelopes will be addressed

Superintendent G. Dixon,
———— Constabulary;

G. Dixon, Esq., Q.P.M.,
Chief Superintendent, Metropolitan
Police;

Below these ranks, the rank is always used before the name, and on envelopes the Force follows the name.

Prime Ministers

Are Privy Counsellors, and are so addressed, according to rank. The Prime Ministers of many Commonwealth countries are also members of the Privy Council; and the Prime Minister of Canada is addressed as Right Hon. for life by virtue of his office.

Provosts of Scottish Cities

As an Esquire (*see* p. 111), but referred to locally as The Provost, rather than "Mr X". But it should be noted that the Civic Heads

of Edinburgh, Dundee, Aberdeen, and Glasgow are known as
Lord Provost (*see* p. 171).

Queen's Counsel

In all respects as an Esquire (or according to rank), with the
initials Q.C. appended to the name on envelopes. When a
Queen's Counsel is appointed a Circuit Judge he continues to use
the initials, but Judges of the High Court cease to use them.

Recorders

Are addressed as an Esquire, or according to rank.

Recorders are barristers or solicitors; they may be Queen's
Counsel, and if so the initials Q.C. should be added.

On the bench they are addressed as "Your Honour".

Sheriffs

In England, Wales and Northern Ireland Sheriffs are appointed,
as officials of the Crown historically concerned with the adminis-
tration of justice, in all counties and in some cities, including the
City of London. Sheriffs of counties are known as High Sheriffs,
indicating that theirs is a senior appointment. The office of Sheriff
requires no special form of address in writing, but may be added
after the name on an envelope when writing on official business:

> Colonel J. C. W. Browne, D.S.O.,
> High Sheriff of ————— shire.

In speech they may be addressed as High Sheriff (of counties), or
Sheriff or Mr Sheriff (of cities), on formal occasions.

In Scotland Sheriffs are Judges of the Sheriff Courts. There are
six Sheriffs-Principal, and within each of their jurisdictions a
number of Sheriffs. All are addressed in court as My Lord.
Otherwise, officially and socially, as Sheriff —————, but the
Sheriff-Principal is referred to as the Sheriff-Principal of —————,

using the first territorial name of conjoined shrievalties, and is so announced.

Stipendiary Magistrates

The same rules are followed as for Justices of the Peace, except that the letters J.P. are not used for stipendiary magistrates.

Vice Lord-Lieutenants

are addressed according to name and rank. The abbreviation V.L. following the name is not used.

ORDERS, DECORATIONS AND HONOURS

Victoria Cross

The Victoria Cross is the most distinguished of all decorations, and is conferred for valour in all branches of the fighting services. Since 1920 it has been extended to include women. The abbreviation V.C. takes precedence of all other decorations and honours.

Other service decorations may be used in accordance with the table on page 179 in addressing a recipient in writing.

George Cross

The George Cross is awarded for acts of great heroism or of conspicuous courage in extreme danger. It is intended primarily for civilians (both men and women), but awards are also made to members of the fighting services in actions for which military honours are not normally granted. The abbreviation G.C. follows V.C. but takes precedence of all other decorations and honours.

Order of Merit—O.M.

A very distinguished order, limited to twenty-four members, ranking in precedence immediately after Knights Grand Cross of the Order of the Bath.

Order of the Companions of Honour—C.H.

An order limited to sixty-five members, for which women are equally eligible with men. It carries no titles, but holders use the initials C.H. after the name. It ranks in precedence after the 1st Class of the Order of the British Empire.

Orders Exclusively for Women

| THE ROYAL ORDER OF VICTORIA AND ALBERT | V.A. |
| THE IMPERIAL ORDER OF THE CROWN OF INDIA | C.I. |

Order of Decorations and Honours

The following list shows the correct order of the various degrees of Honours and Decorations of which the abbreviations are most commonly employed. A higher rank in an order includes the lower, i.e. it is never correct to put G.C.B., K.C.B., or K.C.M.G., C.M.G. All decorations and honours should be given. For the order of letters after the name other than decorations and honours, see pp. 180–182.

(*N.B.*—For the various orders of Knighthood, see pp. 97 to 105.

V.C., G.C., K.G., K.T., K.P., G.C.B., O.M., G.C.S.I., G.C.M.G., G.C.I.E., C.I., G.C.V.O., G.B.E., C.H., .K.C.B., K.C.S.I., K.C.M.G., K.C.I.E., K.C.V.O., K.B.E., C.B., C.S.I., C.M.G., C.I.E., C.V.O., .C.B.E., D.S.O., M.V.O. (4th class), O.B.E., I.S.O., M.V.O. (5th class), M.B.E., R.R.C., D.S.C., M.C., D.F.C., A.F.C., A.R.R.C., A.M., D.C.M., C.G.M., G.M., D.S.M., M.M., D.F.M., A.F.M., Q.G.M., B.E.M., Q.P.M., S.G.M., V.D., E.R.D., T.D., E.D., R.D., V.R.D., A.E.

(For ABBREVIATIONS, see pp. 1–36.)

Various Commonwealth countries have instituted their own orders, which are awarded to their own citizens, and are indicated (in the British fashion) by post-nominal lettering. An example is the Order of Canada, in which three honours are conferred:

> Companion of the Order of Canada (C.C.);
> Officer of the Order of Canada (O.C.);
> Member of the Order of Canada (C.M.).

These letters follow immediately after V.C. or G.C. in their appointed order, for Canadian citizens; and the letters of similar orders in other countries will likewise precede, for their own citizens, any others. In the case of the Order of Australia, however, the grades of the order:

Knight (or Dame) of the Order of Australia (A.K., A.D.);
Companion of the Order of Australia (A.C.);
Officer of the Order of Australia (A.O.);
Member of the Order of Australia (A.M.)

follow respectively O.M., G.B.E., K.B.E., and D.S.O.

In the case of the Queen's Service Order of New Zealand, the letters Q.S.O. precede O.B.E., and Q.S.M. (Queen's Service Medal) follow Q.G.M.

Such orders may be conferred on British subjects who have in some way served another country of the Commonwealth. It is customary to use the letters or distinguishing titles of such orders while in the country which conferred them, but not elsewhere.

Honorific and other affixes

Honorific affixes, whether military decorations or not, should be appended in addressing formal letters; but those that are not honorific should be omitted. D.L. and J.P. are normally omitted in social usage. In no circumstances do honorific initials (even V.C.) appear on visiting cards.

Affixes indicating professional qualification or official status should be used when addressing the correspondent in his professional or official capacity.

The order of lettering after the name (and after the abbreviations Bt. or Esq., if they apply), is fixed, and should be followed:

First, decorations and honours, in the order given on p. 179. They should not be omitted, if any letters are used at all, and in most circumstances it is preferable to include them in an address.

Second, the initials denoting certain Royal appointments, and some made on behalf of the Queen. If for any reason it is necessary to include the initials P.C. they will come first, followed by A.D.C., Q.H.P., Q.H.S., Q.H.D.S., Q.H.N.S., Q.H.C., Q.C., J.P., D.L. It should be noted, however, that P.C. is nowadays never used on envelopes, and that the next appointments (up to Q.H.C.), being short-term ones, are not normally used in ordinary correspondence, although they may be in official letters; Q.C. must always be used; and J.P. and D.L. are used when writing on business connected with the appointment.

Third, University degrees (*see* p. 186).

Fourth, letters, other than university degrees, denoting medical qualifications; in normal correspondence, only those indicating fellowships or memberships would be used. F.R.C.P. and F.R.C.S. should always appear (in that order) if held, and so should the fellowships or memberships of the other institutions conferring postgraduate qualifications; medical precede surgical, which are followed by more specialized fellowships.

Fifth, the fellowships or memberships of learned societies, academies, or professional institutions. As a general rule, these should be shown in the order of the foundation of the societies, etc.; no distinction is made, in the order, between fellowships and memberships. The professional institutions whose highest rank was "member" are however changing this to "fellow"; except in professional correspondence, only these higher ranks would normally be shown. Those fellowships, etc., election to which is a distinction should be used in all correspondence: F.R.S., R.A. or A.R.A., R.S.A., F.B.A., are examples. Others which indicate merely that the fellow declares his interest in and support for the body concerned are used when the subject of his interest is the matter of the correspondence; and those which indicate professional eminence or qualification when writing on professional matters. The members of the sixteen bodies which make up the Council of Engineering Institutions are chartered engineers; they are entitled to use the letters C.Eng., which are placed immediately before the first fellowship or membership giving the right to use them:

J. B. MacTavish, Esq., C.Eng., M.I.C.E., F.I.Mech.E.

Similarly, fellows and members of the Royal Society of Chemistry are entitled to use the abbreviation C.Chem. before the letters F.R.S.C. and M.R.S.C.

Sixth, letters indicating an appointment or office, such as M.P., M.L.A., M.L.C., C.C., W.S.

THE UNIVERSITIES

Chancellors

In speech they are addressed formally as Sir or (in the case of a peer) My Lord or Your Grace as the case may be. More familiarly as Mr Chancellor or Chancellor.

In writing the most formal mode of address is:

> Sir (or according to peerage rank),
>> I am, Sir (My Lord),
>>> Your obedient servant,

Less formally:

> My Lord,   *or*
> Dear Sir,
>> Yours faithfully,

The social manner is:

> Dear Mr Chancellor,   *or*
> Dear Chancellor,
>> Yours sincerely,

Address of envelope in both cases—

> The Rt. Hon. the Earl of Blank,
> Chancellor of the University of ————.

Vice-Chancellors

The rules as for CHANCELLORS apply (Dear Mr Vice-Chancellor, or Dear Vice-Chancellor, etc.) except that the envelope is addressed thus:

The Vice-Chancellor of The University of ————.

The two exceptions to this are Vice-Chancellors of Oxford and Cambridge, who are addressed respectively as:

The Revd. the Vice-Chancellor of The University of Oxford (whether or not he is in Holy Orders)

and

The Right Worshipful the Vice-Chancellor of The University of Cambridge.

The prefix is used only with the office, not with the individual's name.

See also Principals (p. 185).

High Stewards

are addressed in speech according to their rank. In writing the most formal mode is:

> Sir (or according to peerage rank),
> > I am, Sir (My Lord),
> > > Your obedient servant,

Less formally:

> Dear Sir,   *or*
> My Lord,
> > > Yours faithfully,

The social manner is:

> Dear High Steward,
> > Yours sincerely,

> *Address of envelope in both cases—*
> > His Grace the Duke of Blank,
> > High Steward of The University of ————.

Deputy High Stewards

As High Stewards.

Heads of Colleges

May be known as Masters, Mistresses, Presidents, Principals, Provosts, Rectors, or Wardens.

In speech they are addressed formally as Sir or Madam. Socially by name.

In writing they are addressed most formally as:

Sir (or Madam),
                    Your obedient servant,

Less formally:

Dear Sir (or Madam),
                    Yours faithfully,

Socially the address is by name, or (for example)

Dear Master.

Address of envelope in both cases—
          The Master of ————— College, etc.

Deans

of colleges are addressed according to their own name and rank. In the rare cases (cathedral colleges) where a dean is head he is a dean of the Church of England and must be addressed as such (*see* p. 124).

Principals

The head of a Scottish University may be appointed Principal and Vice-Chancellor, and the heads of the Constituent Colleges of the University of Wales are known as Principals. They are

addressed both in speech and in writing as Principal, under the
same rules as a head of a college.

Professors

The title is used in speech and writing, formally and socially.

Most formally:

> Dear Sir (or Madam),
> > I am, dear Sir (or Madam),
> > > Your obedient servant,

Less formally:

> Dear Sir (or Madam),
> > Yours faithfully,

Socially:

> Dear Professor Dash,
> > Yours sincerely,

Address of envelope in all cases—

> Professor J. G. Dash.

Ordained Professors

An ordained professor is referred and spoken to in speech and
writing as Professor Blank. He should be addressed on envelopes,
both formally and socially, as The Revd. Professor W. L. Blank.
If he is a Canon he is addressed as such (*see* p. 127). Such
accumulations as Professor the Revd. Canon ————, though
not unknown are undesirable.

Degrees

The custom established and used by the older universities is
really the best to follow. The rule is that doctors in any faculty use
the designation, while lower degrees (e.g. M.A., LL.B., B.Sc.,

etc.) are omitted, except in circumstances where *all* academic qualifications are appropriate. Even then only the higher of two degrees in the same faculty would be used. Outside academic circles even doctorates would not be appended to the name in a social letter, although of course anyone customarily known as Dr ——————— would still be so. It is a matter of individual choice whether the holder of a doctorate is addressed as Dr ——————— or as John ———————, Esq., with the appropriate lettering, except that it is now the custom always to write the letters D.D. (*See also* Doctors of Medicine, p. 188.) It is never correct to write Dr ———————, Ph.D. (or whatever the lettering might be).

Doctors

Degrees are given by the older and most of the newer universities in seven faculties: Divinity, Law, Literature, Medicine, Music, Philosophy and Science. The following are the various styles and abbreviations:

Doctor of Divinity	D.D.
Doctor of Laws	LL.D.

Conferred by Cambridge and all other universities granting degrees in this faculty.

Doctor of Civil Law	D.C.L.

This is the Oxford, Durham and Newcastle upon Tyne degree corresponding to the Cambridge LL.D.

Doctor of Literature ⎫	Litt.D. (Cambridge, Dublin and
Doctor of Letters ⎭	Liverpool.)
	D.Litt. (Oxford and some others)
	D.Lit. (London and Manchester)
Doctor of Medicine	M.D. (all universities except Oxford)
	D.M. (Oxford University)
Doctor of Music	Mus.D. (Cambridge and Durham)
	D.Mus. (Oxford)
Doctor of Philosophy	Ph.D. (Cambridge and others)
	D.Phil. (Oxford)

DOCTOR OF SCIENCE   Sc.D. (Cambridge and Dublin)
                         D.Sc. (Oxford and others)

Doctors of Medicine

The title has become so wedded to the medical profession that the reminder is needed that not all qualified medical men hold the final degree. Those who do are addressed and referred to in speech as Dr Gray, and letters are addressed:

Thomas Gray, Esq., M.D.

(but in Scotland more usually, Dr Thomas Gray).

If a knighthood or baronetcy has been conferred, the address in speech becomes Sir Thomas Gray or Sir Thomas, and the envelope would be inscribed:

Sir Thomas Gray, M.D.,   or
Sir Thomas Gray, Bt., M.D.

If a peerage has been conferred the address in speech and writing is according to rank (*see* under appropriate headings) with perhaps the degree of medicine added after the more important honours.

Those medical men who have not taken the final degree are addressed in every way as if they have, excepting that their actual qualifications, such as M.B., L.R.C.P., would be substituted for M.D. on the envelope, or, as is normal with general practitioners, they are called simply Dr ————.

There is also the firmly established custom in the medical profession of addressing surgeons both in speech and writing as Mr, and inscribing the envelope thus:

T. Gray, Esq., F.R.C.S.

Gynaecologists tend to be addressed as surgeons in England and Wales, as doctors elsewhere.

Doctors of Divinity

are usually but not always clergymen. The degree can, in some Universities, be taken by, or conferred on, laymen as well. In the case of the clergy, they are addressed and referred to in speech as Dr Read. Formal letters would begin Reverend Sir; social ones, Dear Dr Read, and the envelope in each case would be addressed:

The Revd. J. L. Read, D.D.

Honorary Doctorates

The same rules for use apply as to other holders, although it is not usual to add them if there are other letters after the name already, except in the most comprehensive lists; and they are of course not used in circumstances where they might seem to imply an academic qualification. Many holders of honorary doctorates do enjoy the use of the title Doctor, and their preference should be followed.

Lesser Degrees

Letters denoting masters' and bachelors' degrees, which are, of course, most common, are not used even in university circles in ordinary correspondence, and socially they are not used at all. There are certain formal occasions on which members of learned professions would use them, such as in lists of lectures, etc., but a master's or bachelor's degree would not be appended to a doctor's. The reason for this is that in the older universities a doctor's degree is considered to include an M.A.—it can only very rarely be taken without it.

MASTER OF ARTS	M.A.
BACHELOR OF ARTS	B.A.
BACHELOR OF LETTERS	B.Litt.
BACHELOR OF DIVINITY	B.D.

MASTER OF LAWS	LL.M.
BACHELOR OF LAWS	LL.B.
BACHELOR OF CIVIL LAW	B.C.L.
BACHELOR OF MEDICINE	M.B.
BACHELOR OF MEDICINE	B.M. (Oxford)
BACHELOR OF MUSIC	⎧ B.Mus. ⎨ Mus.B. ⎩ Mus.Bac.
BACHELOR OF SCIENCE	B.Sc.

SOME PRONUNCIATIONS OF PROPER NAMES

a	as in cat
ah	as in father
ay	as in day
g	as in good
i	as in pin
ō	as in home

o	as in dog
ōō	as in food
oo	as in hood
ow	as in how
y	as in spy

Abergavenny — {Aber-ga-*ven*-i (town) / Aber-*gen*-i (title).
Abinger — *Ab*-binjer.
Acheson — *Ach*-ison.
Achonry — *Acon*-ri.
Ackroyd — *Ak*-roid.
Agate — *Ay*-gat.
Ailesbury — *Ayls*-bri.
Ailsa — *Ayl*-sa.
Aitchison — *Aych*-ison.
Akerman — *Ack*-erman.
Akers-Douglas — *Ay*-kers-*Dug*-glas.
Alcester — *Aw*-ster.
Aldenham — *Awl*-dnam.
Alington — *Al*-ington.
Alleyne — *Al*-leen, Al-*lane*, *Al*-len.
Allhusen — Al-*hew*-sen.
Alnemouth — *Ayl*-mouth.
Alnwick — *An*-nick.
Alresford — *Awl*-sford.
Althorp — *Awl*-trup.
Altrincham — *Awl*-tringam.
Amory — *A*-mori.
Ampthill — *Amt*-hill.
Annaly — *An*-nali.
Annesley — *An*-sli.
Anstruther — *An*-struther.
Antrobus — *An*-trobus.
Arbuthnott — Ar-*buth*-not.
Archdall — *Arch*-dale.
Ardagh — *Ar*-da.
Ardee — Ar-*dee*.

Argyll — Ar-*gyle*.
Armagh — Ar-*mah*.
Ashburnham — *Ash*-burnam.
Ashburton — *Ash*-burton.
Ashcombe — *Ash*-com.
Assheton — *Ash*-ton.
Atherton — *Ath*-erton.
Athlumney — Ath-*lum*-ni.
Atholl — *Ath*-ol.
Auchinleck — {*Aff*-leck. / *Awk*-inleck.
Auchterlonie — Aukh-ter-*lōn*-i.
Ava — *Ah*-va.
Ayers — Airs

Baden-Powell — *Bay*-dn-*Pō*-ell.
Bagehot — *Baj*-jut.
Baggallay — *Bag*-gali.
Balcarres — Bal-*car*-riss.
Baldry — *Bawl*-dri.
Balfour — *Bal*-four.
Balgonie — Bal-*gō*-ni.
Balogh — Ballog.
Bamfyld — *Bam*-feeld.
Barham — *Bah*-ram.
Barnardiston — Barnar-*dis*-ton.
Barraclough — *Bar*-racluff.
Barttelot — *Bart*-ilot.
Barwick — *Bar*-rick, also as spelt.
Bateson — *Bayt*-son.
Battye — *Bat*-ti.

191

Baugh	Baw.
Beaconsfield	*Beck*-onsfield (town).
	Bee-consfield (title).
Beatty	*Bee*-ti.
Beauchamp	*Bee*-cham.
Beauclerc/k	*Bō*-clare.
Beaufort	*Bō*-fort.
Beaulieu	*Bew*-li.
Beaumont	*Bō*-mont.
Belisha	Be-*lee*-sha.
Bellamy	*Bel*-lami.
Bellew	*Bell*-yew.
	Bell-*oo*.
Bellingham	*Bell*-injam.
	Bell-ingam.
Belvoir	*Bee*-ver.
Berkeley	*Bark*-li.
Berkshire	*Bark*-shere.
Berners	*Ber*-ners.
Bertie	*Bar*-ti.
Besley	*Beez*-li.
	Bez-li.
Bessborough	*Bez*-burra.
Bethune	*Bee*-ton.
Bicester	*Bis*-ter.
Biddulph	*Bid*-dulf.
Bigelow	*Big*-gelo.
Bispham	*Bis*-pam.
Blakiston	*Black*-iston.
Blois	Bloyce.
Blomefield	B*loom*-field.
Blomfield	
Blount	Blunt.
Blyth	Bly.
	Blyth.
Bois	Boyce.
Boleyn	*Boo*-len.
	Bo-*linn*.
Bolingbroke	*Bol*-linbrook.
Bolitho	By-*ly*-tho.
Bompas	*Bum*-pas.
Bonsor	*Bon*-sor.
Boord	Bord.
Borrowes	*Bur*-roze.
Borthwick	*Borth*-wick.
Bosanquet	*Bōzn*-ket.

Boscawen	Bo-*scō*-en.
	Bo-*scaw*-en.
Bosham	*Boz*-um.
Boughey	*Bow*-i.
Boughton	*Bow*-ton.
	Baw-ton.
Bourchier	*Bow*-cher.
Bourke	Berk.
Bourne	Born.
	Bern.
	Bourn.
Bowles	Boles.
Brabazon	*Brab*-bazon.
Brabourne	*Bray*-bn.
Breadalbane	Bred-*awl*-ban.
Brechin	*Breek*-hin.
Broke	Brook.
Brough	Bruff.
Brougham	Broom.
Broughton	*Braw*-ton.
Buccleuch	Bu-*cloo*.
Buchan	*Buk*-han.
Buchanan	Bu-*can*-non.
Burbury	*Ber*-bery.
Burges	*Ber*-jez.
Burghclere	*Ber*-clair.
Burghersh	*Ber*-gersh.
Burghley	*Ber*-li.
Burroughes	*Bur*-roze.
Bury	*Ber*-ri.
	Bew-ri.
Caccia	Katcha.
Cadogan	Ka-*dug*-gan.
Cahill	*Kay*-hill.
Caillard	*Ky*-ar.
Caius	Kees
Calderon	*Kawld*-eron.
Callaghan	*Kall*-ahan.
	Kall-igan
Calthorpe	*Kawl*-thorp.
Camoys	Kam-*oys*.
Campden	*Kam*-den.
Capell	*Kay*-pel.
Carbery	*Kar*-beri.

Carew	*Kair*-i.
	Kar-*oo*.
Carlyon	Kar-*ly*-on.
Carmichael	Kar-*my*-kal.
Carnegie	Kar-*neg*-gi.
Carnwath	*Karn*-woth.
Carpmael	*Karp*-male.
Carruthers	Kar-*ruth*-ers.
Carshalton	Kar-*shaw*-ton.
Cassilis	*Kas*-sels.
Castlereagh	*Kah*-selray.
Cavan	*Kav*-van.
Cavanagh	*Kav*-vana.
Chalmers	*Chah*-mers.
Chaloner	*Chal*-loner.
Chandos	*Shan*-dos.
Charlemont	*Charl*-mon.
Charteris	*Char*-teris.
	Char-ters.
Cheetham	*Cheet*-am.
Cherwell	*Char*-well.
Chetwode	*Chet*-wood.
Chetwynd	*Chet*-wind.
Cheylesmore	*Chil*-smor.
Cheyne	*Chay*-ni.
Chichele	*Chich*-eli.
	Chi-*chailey*.
Chisholm	*Chiz*-zom.
Chiswick	*Chiz*-ik.
Cholmeley	
Cholmondeley	*Chum*-li.
Chomley	
Cirencester	*Syr*-ensester.
Clanricarde	Klan-*rick*-ard.
Clarina	Kla-*reen*-a.
Claverhouse	*Klay*-vers, also as
	spelt.
Clerk	Klark.
Clerke	Klark.
Cliveden	*Kliv*-den.
Clogher	Klo-her.
Cloncurry	Klun-*cur*-ri.
Clonmell	Klon-*mel*.
Clough	Kluff.
Clowes	Klews.
	Klows.

Clwyd	*Klew*-id.
Cochrane	*Kock*-ran.
Cockburn	*Ko*-burn.
Coghill	*Kog*-hill.
Coke	Kook.
	Koke.
Colborne	*Kole*-burn.
Colles	*Kol*-lis.
Colquhoun	Ko-*hoon*.
Colville	*Koll*-vil.
	Koal-vil.
Combe	Koom.
Compton	*Kump*-ton.
Conisborough	*Kun*-sbra.
Constable	*Kun*-stable.
Conyngham	*Kun*-ningam.
Copleston	*Kop*-pelston.
Corcoran	*Kork*-ran.
Cottenham	*Kot*-tenam
Cottesloe	*Kot*-slo.
Couch	Kōōch.
Courtenay	
Courtney	*Kort*-ni.
Courthope	*Kort*-ope.
Courtown	*Kor*-town.
Cousens	*Kuz*-zens.
Coutts	Kōōts.
Coventry	*Kov*-entri.
	Kuv-entri.
Coverdale	*Kuv*-erdale.
Coverley	*Kuv*-erli.
Cowell	*Kow*-ell.
	Kō-ell.
Cowen	*Kō*-en.
	*Kow*en.
Cowles	Koles.
Cowper	*Kōō*-per.
	Kow-per.
Cozens	*Kuz*-zens.
Craigavon	Craig-*a*-von.
Craster	*Crah*-ster
Crawshay	*Kraw*-shay.
Creagh	Kray.
Creighton	*Kry*-ton.
Crespigny	*Krep*-ni.
Crichton	*Kry*-ton.

Croghan	*Krō*-an.	D'Eyncourt	Dain-curt.
Cromartie	*Krum*-marti.	De Zoete	De Zōōt.
Crombie	*Krum*-bi.	Dillwyn	*Dil*-lon.
Culme-Seymour	*Kulm-See*-mer.	Disraeli	Diz-*rail*-i.
Cuningham ⎫		Donegal	*Don*-igawl.
Cuninghame ⎬	*Kun*-ningam.	Doneraile	*Dun*-erayl.
Cunyngham ⎭		Donoghue	*Dun*-nohoo.
		Donoughmore	*Dun*-nomor.
Dacre	*Day*-ker.	Dougall	*Doo*-gal.
Dacres	*Day*-kers.	Doughty	*Dow*-ti.
Dahrendorf	*Darr*-endorf.	Douglas	*Dug*-las.
Dalbiac	*Dawl*-biac.	Drogheda	*Draw*-eda.
Dalgleish	Dal-*gleesh*.	Du Cane	Dew *Kane*.
Dalhousie	Dal-*how*-zi.	Duchesne	Du-*kahn*.
Dalmeny	Dal-*men*-ni.	Ducie	*Dew*-ssi.
Dalrymple	Dal-*rim*-ple.	Dumaresq	Doo-*mer*-rick.
Dalziel	⎰ Dee-*ell*.	Dumfries	Dum-*freess*.
	⎱ Dal-*zeel*.	Dunalley	Dun-*nal*-li.
Daubeney	*Daw*-bni.	Dundas	Dun-*das*.
Daventry	As spelt.	Dungarvan	Dun-*gar*-van.
Death	De-*ath*.	Dunglass	Dun-*glass*.
De Burgh	De Berg.	Dunmore	Dun-*mor*.
Decies	*Dee*-shees.	Dunsany	Dun-*sa*-ni.
De Crespigny	De *Krep*-ni.	Duntze	Dunts.
De Hoghton	De Horton.	Dupplin	*Dup*-plin.
De la Poer	De la Poor.	Du Quesne	Dew *Kane*.
De la Warr	*De*-lawar.	Durand	Dew-*rand*.
De l'Isle	De Lyle.	Durrant	⎰ Dur-*rant*.
De Moleyns	*Dem*-moleens.		⎱ *Dur*-rant.
De Mont-		Dwyfor	*Dwy*-for.
morency	De Muntmor-*en*-si.	Dymoke	*Dim*-muk.
Denbigh	*Den*-bi.	Dynevor	*Din*-nevor.
Derby	*Dar*-bi.	Dysart	*Dy*-sart.
Dering	*Deer*-ing.		
De Rohan	De *Ro*-an.	Eardley-Wilmot	*Erd*-li-*Wil*-mot.
De Ros	De Roos.	Ebrington	*Ebb*-rington.
Derwent	*Dar*-went, also as	Ebury	*Ee*-beri.
	spelt.	Edgcumbe	*Ej*-cum.
De Salis	⎰ De *Sal*-lis.	Edwardes	Edwards.
	⎱ De Sahls.	Egerton	*Ej*-erton.
De Saumarez ⎫		Elam	*Ee*-lam.
De Sausmarez ⎭	De *So*-marez.	Elcho	*El*-ko.
Devereux	⎰ *Dev*-veroo.	Elibank	*El*-libank.
	⎱ *Dev*-veroox.	Eliot	*Ell*-iot.
De Vesci	De *Vess*-i.	Ellesmere	*Els*-meer.

Elphinstone	*El*-finston.
Elwes	El-*weez*.
Enniskillen	*In*-nis-*kil*-len.
Ernle	*Ern*-li.
Esmonde	*Ez*-mond.
Etheredge	*Eth*-erij.
Evershed	*Ev*-ershed.
Ewart	*U*-art.
Eyre	Air.
Eyton	*Y*-ton.
Falconbridge	*Fawk*-onbrij.
Falconer	*Fawk*-ner.
Falkland	*Fawk*-land.
Farquhar	{ *Fark*-wer. { *Fark*-er.
Farquharson	{ *Fark*-werson. { *Fark*-erson.
Fawcett	{ *Faw*-set. { *Foss*-et.
Featherston- haugh	*Feth*-erstonhaw.
Feilden	*Feel*-den.
Feilding	*Feel*-ding.
Fenwick	*Fen*-ick.
Fermanagh	*Fer*-mana.
Feversham	*Fav*-ersham.
Ffolkes	Fokes.
Ffoulkes	{ Fokes. { Fōōks.
Fiennes	Fynes.
Findlater	*Fin*-litter.
Findlay	*Fin*-li.
Fingall	*Fin*-gawl.
Fitzhardinge	Fitz-*hard*-ing.
Fleming	*Flem*-ming.
Foljambe	*Fool*-jam.
Forbes	Forbs.
Fortescue	*Fort*-iskew.
Foulis	Fowls.
Fowey	Foy.
Fowke	Foke.
Freake	Freek.
Fremantle	Free-*man*-tle.
Freyer	{ *Free*-ar. { *Fry*-er.

Froude	Frōōd.
Furneaux	*Fur*-no.
Gairdner	*Gard*-ner.
Galbraith	Gal-*brayth*.
Gallagher	*Gal*-laher.
Gallwey Galway	} *Gawl*-way.
Garmoyle	Gar-*moyl*.
Garnock	*Gar*-nock.
Garvagh	*Gar*-va.
Gatacre	*Gat*-taker.
Gathorne	*Gay*-thorn.
Geddes	*Ged*-diz.
Gee	{ Gee. { Jee.
Geikie	*Gee*-ki.
Gell	{ Gell. { Jell.
Geoghegan	*Gay*-gun.
Gerard	*Jer*-rard.
Gervis-Meyrick	*Jer*-vis-*Mer*-ick.
Gethen Gethin Gething	} *Geth*-in. *Geeth*-in.
Gibbes	Gibbs.
Giddens	*Gid*-dens.
Giffard	{ *Gif*-fard. { *Jif*-fard.
Gilhooly	Gil-*hoo*-li.
Gilkes	Jilks.
Gill	{ Gill. { Jill.
Gilles	*Gill*-is.
Gillespie	Gill-*ess*-pi.
Gillingham	{ *Jill*-ingam. (Kent). { *Gill*-ingam (Dorset).
Gilmour	*Gil*-mor.
Gilroy	*Gil*-roy.
Glamis	Glahms.
Glerawly	Gler-*aw*-li.
Goldsworthy	*Gōls*-worthi.
Gomme	Gom.
Gorges	*Gor*-jiz.

Gormanston	*Gor*-manston.
Goschen	*Gō*-shen.
Gough	Goff.
Goulburn	*Gōōl*-burn.
Gourley	*Goor*-li.
Gower	Gaw, also as spelt.
Graeme	Grame.
Graham ⎫	
Grahame ⎭	*Gray*-am.
Granard	*Gran*-nard.
Greaves	⎰ Graves.
	⎱ Greeves.
Greenhalgh	⎰ *Green*-how.
	⎱ *Green*-haltch.
Greig	Greg.
Greville	*Grev*-el.
Grier	Greer.
Grosvenor	*Grove*-nor.
Guildford	*Gil*-ford.
Guinness	*Gin*-iss.
Gwatkin	*Gwot*-kin.
Gwynedd	*Gwin*-eth.
Gye	Jy.
Haden	*Hay*-dn.
Haggard	*Hag*-gard.
Haigh	Hayg.
Haldane	*Hawl*-dane.
Haldon	*Hawl*-don.
Hallé	*Hal*-lay.
Halsbury	*Hawl*-sbri.
Halsey	⎰ *Hawl*-si.
	⎱ *Hal*-si.
Hamond	*Ham*-mond.
Hampden	*Ham*-den.
Hanbury	*Han*-buri.
Harberton	*Har*-berton.
Harcourt	*Har*-curt.
Hardinge	*Har*-ding.
Harewood	*Har*-wood.
Harington	*Ha*-rington.
Harlech	*Har*-lick.
Hawarden	⎰ *Hay*-warden.
	⎱ *Har*-den.
Headlam	*Hed*-lam.
Heathcote	*Heth*-cot.

Hegarty	*Heg*-arti.
Heneage	*Hen*-ij.
Hennessey ⎫	
Hennessy ⎭	*Hen*-essi.
Henniker	*Hen*-iker.
Henriques	Hen-*reek*-iz.
Hepburn	*Heb*-burn.
Herries	*Her*-ris.
Herschell	*Her*-shel.
Hertford	*Har*-ford.
Hervey	⎰ *Her*-vi.
	⎱ *Har*-vi.
Heytesbury	*Hayt*-sburi.
Hindlip	*Hind*-lip.
Hobart	⎰ *Hō*-bart.
	⎱ *Hub*-bart.
Holbech	*Hol*-beech.
Holmes	Homes.
Holmesdale	*Home*-sdale.
Holm-Patrick	Home-Patrick.
Home	Hume, also as spelt.
Honyman	*Hun*-niman.
Honywood	*Hun*-niwood.
Hopetoun	*Hope*-ton.
Hotham	*Huth*-am.
Hough	Huff.
Houghton	⎧ Huf-ton.
	⎪ *Haw*-ton.
	⎨ *How*-ton.
	⎩ *Ho*-ton.
Houston	*Hoost*-on.
Howorth	*How*-erth.
Hugessen	⎰ *Hew*-jessen.
	⎱ *Hew*-gessen.
Huish	*Hew*-ish.
Humphrey	*Hum*-fri.
Hunstanton	*Hun*-ston, or as spelt.
Hyndman	*Hynd*-man.
Iddesleigh	*Id*-sli.
Ightham	*Y*-tam.
Inchiquin	*Inch*-quin.
Inge	Ing.
Ingelow	*In*-jelow.

Ingestre	*In*-gestri.	Kirkcudbright	Kirk-*oo*-bri.
Ingham	*Ing*-am.	Knightly	*Nyt*-ly.
Inglis	*In*-gools, or as	Knighton	*Ny*-ton.
	spelt.	Knollys ⎫	
Innes	*In*-nis.	Knowles ⎭	Noles.
Inveraray	Inver-*air*-i.	Knutsford	*Nuts*-ford.
Inverarity	Inver-*arr*-iti.	Kynaston	*Kin*-naston.
Isitt	*Y*-sit.		
Iveagh	*Y*-va.	Lacon	*Lay*-kon.
		Laffan	La-*ffan*.
Jacoby	*Jack*-obi.	Langrishe	*Lang*-rish.
Jeaffreson	*Jeff*-erson.	Larpent	*Lar*-pent.
Jeffreys	*Jef*-riz.	Lascelles	*Las*-sels.
Jerome	Jer-*ome*.	Lathom	*Lay*-thom.
Jervaulx	*Jer*-vis.	Laughton	*Law*-ton.
	⎧ *Jar*-vis.	Lavengro	*Lav*-engro.
Jervis	⎨	Lawrence	*Lor*-rence.
	⎩ *Jer*-vis.	Layard	Laird, or as
Jervois	*Jar*-vis.		spelt.
Jeune	Joon.	Lea	Lee.
Jeyes	Jays.	Learmonth	*Ler*-munth.
Jocelyn	*Joss*-lin.	Leatham	*Leeth*-am.
Jolliffe	*Joll*-if.		⎧ Leeths.
Julyan	*Jōō*-lian.	Leathes	⎨
			⎩ *Leeth*-iz.
		Lechmere	*Leech*-meer.
Kaberry	*Kay*-berry.	Leconfield	*Lek*-onfield.
Keatinge	*Keet*-ing.		⎧ *Leff*-enyu.
Keighley	*Keeth*-li.	Le Fanu	⎨
Keightley	*Keet*-li.		⎩ *Leff*-noo.
Keiller	*Kee*-ler.	Lefevre	Le-*fee*-ver.
Kekewich	*Keck*-wich.	Lefroy	Le-*froy*.
Kennard	Ken-ard.	Legard	*Lej*-ard.
Kenyon	*Ken*-ion.	Legge	Leg.
Keogh ⎫		Legh	Lee.
Keough ⎬	*Kee*-ō.	Lehmann	*Lay*-man.
Kehoe ⎭		Leicester	*Lest*-er.
Kesteven	*Kest*-even.	Leigh	Lee.
	⎧ Kayns.	Leighton	*Lay*-ton.
Keynes	⎨		⎧ *Len*-ster.
	⎩ Keens.	Leinster	⎨
Killanin	Kill-*an*-in.		⎩ *Lin*-ster.
Kilmorey	Kil-*mur*-ri.	Leishman	*Leesh*-man.
Kincairney	Kin-*cair*-ni.	Leitrim	*Leet*-rim.
Kingscote	*Kings*-cut.	Lemesurier	Le-*mézu*rer.
Kinnaird	Kin-*naird*.	Leominster	*Lem*-ster.
Kinnear	Kin-*near*.	Le Patourel	Le-*pat*-turel.
Kinnoull	Kin-*nool*.	Le Poer	Le-*por*.
		Le Queux	Le *Kew*.

Leven	*Lee*-ven.
Leverhulme	*Lee*-verhewm.
Leveson-Gower	*Lōō*-son-Gaw.
Levey	{ *Lee*-vi. / *Lev*-vi.
Ley	Lee.
Leyland	*Lay*-land.
Liardet	*Lee*-ardet
Lingen	*Ling*-en.
Lisle	{ Lyle. / Leel.
Listowel	Lis-*tō*-el.
Llangattock	Klan-*gat*-tock.
Llewellyn	Loo-*ell*-in.
Lochiel	Lok-*heel*.
Logue	Lōg.
Lough	Luff.
Loughborough	*Luf*-burra.
Lovat	*Luv*-at.
Lovibond	*Luv*-band, also as spelt.
Lowther	*Low*-ther.
Lugard	Loo-*gard*.
Lygon	*Lig*-gon.
Lymington	*Lim*-mington.
Lympne	Lim.
Lynam	*Ly*-nam.
Lysaght	*Ly*-sat or *Ly*-sacht.
Lysons	*Ly*-sons.
Lyveden	*Liv*-den.
Macalister	Mac-*al*-ister.
Macara	Mac-*ah*-ra.
McCorquodale	Ma-*cork*-odale.
Maccullagh	Ma-*cul*-la.
M'Culloch	Ma-*cul*-lokh.
M'Eachern	Mac-*kek*-run.
McEvoy	*Mack*-evoy.
M'Ewan / MacEwen	Mac-*kew*-an.
M'Gee / M'Ghee	Ma-*gee*.
MacGillivray	Ma-*gil*-veri.
M'Gillycuddy	*Mack*-licuddi.
Machell	*May*-chell.
Machen	*May*-chen.

M'Ilwraith	*Mack*-ilrayth.
MacIver / M'Ivor	Mack-y-ver.
McKay	Mac-*ky*.
Mackie	*Mack*-i.
Maclachlan	Mac-*laukh*-lan.
Maclagan	Mac-*lag*-gan.
Maclaren	Mac-*lar*-ren.
Maclean	Ma-clayn.
Macleay	Ma-*clay*.
Macleod	Ma-*clowd*.
Macmahon	Mac-*mahn* (with internal h).
Macnamara	Macna-*mah*-ra.
M'Naught	Mac-*nawt*.
MacNaughton	Mac-*naw*-ton.
Macneill	Mac-*neel*.
Maconchy	Ma-*conk*-i.
Maconochie	Mack-*on*-okhi.
Magdalen(e)	*Mawd*-lin.
Magrath	Ma-*grah*.
Maguire	Ma-*gwire*.
Mahon	{ Mahn. / Ma-*hoon*.
Mahony	{ *Mah*-ni. / Ma-hōn-i.
Mainwaring	*Man*-nering.
Majendie	*Maj*-endi.
Malet	*Mal*-let.
Mall, The	Mal, The.
Malmesbury	*Mahm*-sbri.
Mansergh	*Man*-zer.
Marjoribanks	*March*-banks.
Marlborough	*Mawl*-bra.
Martineau	*Mart*-ino.
Masham	*Mass*-am.
Maskelyne	*Mask*-elin.
Massereena	Ma*zereena.
Mather	{ *May*-ther. / *Math*-er.
Matheson	{ *Math*-ison. / *Mat*-tison.
Maugham	Mawm.
Maughan	Mawn.
Maunsell	*Man*-sell.
Maurice	*Mor*-ris.

Mayo	*May*-o.
Meath	Meeth.
Meiklejohn	*Mick*-eljon.
Meldrum	*Mel*-drum.
Melhuish	*Mel*-lish.
Menzies	*Meng*-iz. / *Menz*-iz. / *Ming*-iz.
Meopham	*Mep*-pam. / *Meff*-am.
Mereworth	*Merri*-worth.
Meux	Mewz.
Meyer	*My*-er.
Meynell	*Men*-nel.
Meyrick	*Mer*-rick.
Meysey-Thompson	*May*-zi-*Toms*-on.
Michelham	*Mich*-lam.
Michie	*Mik*-ki.
Midleton	Middleton.
Mildmay	*Myld*-may.
Millard	Mil-*lard*.
Milles	Mills.
Milngavie	Mull-*gy*.
Molyneaux / Molyneux	*Mol*-neux. / *Mol*-new.
Monaghan	*Mon*-nahan.
Monck	Munk.
Monckton	*Munk*-ton.
Moncrieff	Mon-*creef*.
Monkhouse	*Munk*-hows.
Monkswell	*Munk*-swell.
Monro / Monroe	Mun-*ro*.
Monson	*Mun*-son.
Montagu	*Mont*-agew.
Monteagle	Mun-*tee*-gle.
Montefiore	Montifi-*or*-i.
Montgomery	Munt-*gum*-meri.
Monzie	Mun-*ee*.
Moran	*Mor*-an.
Morant	Mo-*rant*.
Moray	*Mur*-ri.
Mordaunt	*Mor*-dunt.
Morice	*Mor*-ris.
Morrell	Murr-ell.
Mostyn	*Moss*-tin.
Mouat	*Moo*-at.
Moule	Mole
Moulton	*Mōl*-ton.
Mountmorres	Mount-*mor*-ris.
Mowat	*Mo*-at. / *Moo*-at.
Mowbray	*Mow*-bri. / *Moo*-bri.
Moynihan	*Moy*-ni-han.
Muncaster	*Mun*-kaster.
Naas	Nace.
Naesmyth	*Nay*-smith.
Napier	*Nay*-pier.
Neave	Neev.
Neil	Neel.
Nepean	Ne-*peen*.
Newburgh	*New*-bra.
Newnes	Newns.
Nigel	*Ny*-jel.
Niven	*Niv*-ven.
Northbourne	*North*-burn.
Northcote	*North*-cot.
Nunburnholme	Nun-*bern*-um.
O'Callaghan	*Ocall*-ahan.
Ochterlony	Octerl-*o*-ni.
O'Donoghue	O-*dun*-nahoo.
Ogilvy	*O*-gelvi.
O'Hagan	*O-hay*-gan.
Olivier	*O-liv*-vier. / *O-liv*-iay.
O'Meara	*O-mah*-ra.
O'Morchoe	*O-mur*-roo.
Onions	O-*ny*-ons. / *Un*-ions.
Ormonde	*Or*-mond.
Osbourne	*Os*-burn.
O'Shaughnessy	O-*shaw*-nessi. / O-*shawk*-nessi.
Outram	*Oo*tram.
Paget	*Paj*-it.
Pakenham	*Pack*-enum.

Palgrave	Pal-grave.		
Parnell	*Par*-nal.		
Pasley	*Pay*-zli.		
Paterson	*Pat*-terson.		
Paton	*Pay*-ton.		
Pauncefote	*Powns*-foot.		
Pease	Peez.		
Pechell	*Pee*-chel.		
Pembroke	*Pem*-brook.		
Pennefather	*Pen*-nifether.		
Pennycuick	{ *Pen*-nicook. / *Pen*-niquick. }		
Penrhyn	Pen-*rin*.		
Pepys	{ Peeps (ancient). / *Pep*-piss (modern). }		
Pery	*Peer*-i.		
Peto	*Pee*-tō.		
Petre	*Pee*-ter.		
Petrie	*Pee*-tri.		
Pierpoint / Pierrepoint	{ Peerpont, also / as spelt. }		
Pigou	Pi-*goo*.		
Pirbright	*Per*-brite.		
Pirie	Pirri.		
Pleydell- Bouverie	*Pled*-el *Boo*-veri.		
Pochin	*Putch*-in.		
Pole	{ Pool. / Pōl. }		
Pole Carew	Pool *Cair*-i.		
Poltimore	*Pol*-timor.		
Polwarth	*Pole*-werth.		
Ponsonby	*Pun*-sunbi.		
Pontefract	*Pum*-fret, also as spelt.		
Portal	*Por*-tal.		
Porteous	*Por*-tius.		
Poulett	*Pau*-let.		
Powell	{ *Po*-ell. / *Pow*-ell. }		
Powerscourt	*Poor*-scort.		
Powlett	*Paw*-let.		
Powys	*Po*-is.		
Praed	Prade.		
Pretyman	*Prit*-timan.		
Prevost	*Prev*-vo.		

Prideaux	{ *Pree*-do. / *Prid*-dux. / *Prid*-do. }
Probyn	*Pro*-bin.
Prothero	*Proth*-ero.
Prowse	Prowz.
Pugh	Pew.
Pwellheli	*Pool*-helli.
Pytchley	*Pych*-li.
Ralegh	{ *Raw*-li. / *Ral*-li. }
Ralph	{ Ralf. / Rafe. }
Ranelagh	*Ran*-ela.
Ranfurly	*Ran*-ferli.
Ranjitsinhji	*Ran*-jit-*sin*-ji.
Rankeillour	Rankiller.
Rashleigh	*Rash*-li.
Rathdonnell	Rath-*don*-nel.
Rathmore	Rath-*mor*.
Rayleigh	*Ray*-li.
Raynham	*Rain*-am.
Reading	*Red*-ing.
Reay	Ray.
Renwick	*Ren*-nick.
Reuter	*Roy*-ter.
Rhondda	*Ron*-tha.
Rhys	{ Rees. / Rice. }
Riddell	*Rid*-dle.
Rievaulx	{ *Riv*-els. / *Reev*-o. }
Robartes	Ro-*barts*.
Roche	Roche.
Rolleston	*Rol*-ston.
Romilly	*Rom*-ili.
Romney	{ *Rum*-ni. / *Rom*-ni. }
Ronaldshay	*Ron*-ald-shay.
Rothes	*Roth*-is.
Rothwell	*Row*-ell.
Rouse	Rouse.
Routh	Rowth.
Roxburghe	*Rox*-bra.

Ruislip	*Ry*-slip.
Ruthven	{ *Riv*-ven. { *Ri*-then.
Sacheverell	Sash-*ev*-erel.
St. Aubyn	S'nt *Aw*-bin.
St. Clair	*Sin*-clair.
St. Cyres	Sin-*seer*.
St. John	*Sin*-jun.
St. Leger	{ *Sil*-linjer. { S'nt *Lej*-er.
St. Maur	{ S'nt *Mor*. { *See*-mer.
St. Neots	S'nt *Neets*.
Salisbury	*Sawl*-sberri.
Saltoun	{ *Sawl*-ton. { *Sal*-ton.
Sandes } Sandys }	Sands.
Sault-St. Marie	*Soo*-St. Marie.
Saumarez	{ *So*-marrez. { *Sum*-mers.
Sausmarez	
Saunders	*Sahn*-ders.
Saunderson	*Sahn*-derson.
Saye and Sele	Say an Seel.
Sayer	Sair.
Scafell	{ *Scaw*-fell. { *Scah*-fell.
Scarborough	*Scar*-burra.
Scarbrough	*Scar*-bra.
Sclater	*Slay*-ter.
Scone	Scoon.
Scrymgeour	*Scrim*-jer.
Searle	Serl.
Sedbergh	*Sed*-ber.
Sempill	*Semp*-il.
Sergeant	*Sar*-jent.
Seton } Setoun }	*See*-ton.
Seymour	{ *See*-mer. { *See*-mor.
Shakerley	*Shak*-erli.
Shearman	*Sher*-man.
Sherborne	{ *Sher*-bern. { *Sher*-born.
Shrewsbury	*Shrō*-sberri.

Sidebotham	*Side*-bottam.
Skrine	Skreen.
Slaithwaite	*Slo*-it, also as spelt.
Smijth	Smythe.
Sodor	*So*-dor.
Somers	*Sum*-mers.
Somerset	*Sum*-erset.
Somerton	*Sum*-merton.
Sondes	Sonds.
Sotherby	*Suth*-ebi.
Southwell	*Su*-thell.
Speight	Spate.
Stalbridge	*Stawl*-bridge.
Stanton	*Stahn*-ton.
Stavordale	*Stay*-vordale.
Stormonth	*Stor*-munth.
Stoughton	{ *Staw*-ton. { *Stow*-ton.
Stourton	*Ster*-ton.
Strachey	*Stray*-chi.
Strahan } Strachan }	Strawn. *Strack*-en.
Stranraer	Stran-*rar*.
Strathallan	Strath-*al*-an.
Strathcona	Strath-*co*-na.
Stratheden	Strath-*ee*-den.
Strathmore	*Strath*-mor.
Stucley	*Stew*-kli.
Sudeley	*Sewd*-li.
Sudley	*Sud*-li.
Suirdale	*Sheur*-dale.
Sweatman	*Swet*-man.
Sweetman	*Sweet*-man.
Symonds	*Sim*-monds.
Symons	*Sim*-mons, also as spelt.
Synge	Sing.
Tangye	*Tang*-i.
Teignmouth	*Tin*-muth.
Tewkesbury	*Tewks*-berri.
Teynham	*Tan*-am.
Thames	Tems.
Theobald	*Tib*-bald, also as spelt.
Thesiger	*Thes*-sijer.

Thorold	*Thur*-uld, also as spelt.	Walsingham	*Wawl*-singam.
		Wantage	*Won*-tij.
Thuillier	*Twil*-lier.	Warburton	*War*-burton.
Thynne	Thin.	Warre	Wor.
Tighe	Ty.	Warwick	*Wor*-rick.
Tollemache	*Tol*-mash.	Wauchope	*Waw*-kup.
Torphichen	Tor-*fick*-en.	Waugh	Waw.
Toynbee	*Toyn*-bi.	Wednesbury	*Wens*-berri.
	⎧ Tra-*fal*-gar	Weir	Weer.
Trafalgar	⎨ (Square).		⎧ *Wel*-sli.
	⎩ Trafal-*gar* (title).	Wellesley	⎨ *Wes*-li.
Traquair	Trak-*ware*.	Wemyss	Weems.
Tredegar	Tred-*ee*-gar.	Westcott	*West*-cot.
Trefusis	Tre-*few*-sis.	Westenra	*West*-enra.
Treloar	Tre-*lor*.	Whalley	*Whay*-li.
Trevelyan	Tre-*vi*-lian.	Wilde	Wyld.
Trewin	Tre-*win*.	Willard	Will-*ard*.
Trimlestown	*Trim*-melston.	Willes	Wills.
Troubridge	*Troo*-bridge.	Willoughby	*Wil*-lobi.
Tuite	Tewt.	Willoughby-	*Wil*-lobi-
Tullibardine	Tulli-*bard*-een.	D'Eresby	Dersbi.
Turnour	*Ter*-ner.	Willoughby de	*Wil*-loby de
Tyrwhitt	*Tir*-rit.	Broke	Brook.
Tyssen	*Ty*-sen.	Winchilsea	*Winch*-elsee.
Tytler	*Tyt*-ler.	Winstanley	*Win*-stanli.
		Woburn	*Woo*-bern.
Uist	*Oo*-ist.	Wodehouse	*Wood*-house.
Urquhart	*Erk*-ert.	Wolcombe	*Wool*-cum.
Uttoxeter	Yew-*tox*-eter.	Wollaston	*Wool*-aston.
		Wolmer	*Wool*-mer.
Vanburgh	*Van*-bra.	Wolseley	*Wool*-sli.
Van Dyck	Van-*dyke*.	Wombwell	*Woom*-well.
Van Straubenzee	Van Straw-*ben*-zie.	Woolwich	*Wool*-ich.
Vaughan	Vawn.	Worcester	*Woos*-ter.
	⎧ Vox.	Worsley	*Wer*-sli.
Vaux	⎨ Vokes.	Wortley	*Wert*-li.
Vavasour	*Vav*-vaser.	Wraxhall	*Rax*-all.
Vesey	*Vee*-zi.	Wreford	*Ree*-ford.
Villiers	*Vil*-lers.	Wrey	Ray.
Vyvyan	*Viv*-vian.		⎧ *Ry*-othsli.
		Wriothesley	⎨ *Rox*-li.
Waldegrave	*Wawl*-grave.	Wrixon	*Rix*-on.
Waleran	*Wawl*-ran.		⎧ *Roo*-tham.
Walford	*Wawl*-ford.	Wrotham	⎨ *Root*-em.
Wallop	*Wol*-lup.	Wrottesley	*Rot*-sli.
Walmesley	*Wawm*-sli.	Wroughton	*Raw*-ton.

Wylie Wyllie }	*Wȳ*-li.	Yeats Yerburgh Yonge	Yayts. *Yar*-burra. Yung.
Yeates Yeatman	Yayts. *Yayt*-man.	Zouche	Zoosh.

INDEX